Propeller Programming

Using Assembler, Spin, and C

Sridhar Anandakrishnan

Apress®

Propeller Programming: Using Assembler, Spin, and C

Sridhar Anandakrishnan
Department of Geosciences, University Park,
Pennsylvania, USA

ISBN-13 (pbk): 978-1-4842-3353-5   ISBN-13 (electronic): 978-1-4842-3354-2
https://doi.org/10.1007/978-1-4842-3354-2

Library of Congress Control Number: 2018935236

Managing Director, Apress Media LLC: Welmoed Spahr
Acquisitions Editor: Natalie Pao
Development Editor: James Markham
Coordinating Editor: Jessica Vakili

Cover designed by eStudioCalamar

Cover image designed by Freepik (www.freepik.com)

Cover photo: Double slip at Munich Central, 2005. Photo by Bjorn Laczay, license CC-BY-SA 2.0. https://goo.gl/q7EHSv.

Distributed to the book trade worldwide by Springer Science+Business Media New York, 233 Spring Street, 6th Floor, New York, NY 10013. Phone 1-800-SPRINGER, fax (201) 348-4505, e-mail orders-ny@springer-sbm.com, or visit www.springeronline.com. Apress Media, LLC is a California LLC and the sole member (owner) is Springer Science + Business Media Finance Inc (SSBM Finance Inc). SSBM Finance Inc is a Delaware corporation.

For information on translations, please e-mail rights@apress.com, or visit www.apress.com/rights-permissions.

Apress titles may be purchased in bulk for academic, corporate, or promotional use. eBook versions and licenses are also available for most titles. For more information, reference our Print and eBook Bulk Sales web page at www.apress.com/bulk-sales.

Any source code or other supplementary material referenced by the author in this book is available to readers on GitHub via the book's product page, located at www.apress.com/9781484233535. For more detailed information, please visit www.apress.com/source-code.

Table of Contents

About the Author

Sridhar Anandakrishnan is a professor of glaciology and geophysics
at Pennsylvania State University where he studies the flow of glaciers in
Antarctica and Greenland. Sridhar uses the Propeller chip in a seismic data
acquisition device that is used "on the ice," as they say!

Acknowledgments

I would like to thank Peter Burkett, Bruce Long, and Don Voigt for their help in the lab and in the field. They designed and deployed rugged and precise instruments in Antarctica and Greenland that helped to shape our knowledge of those continents. I would like to thank the US National Science Foundation, whose financial and logistical support has made this work possible. I would like to thank my wife Martha Bright, whose love and support has made this book possible.

Preface

This book is intended for those who are familiar with Spin programming for the Parallax Propeller microcontroller but who want to learn Propeller C and Propeller Assembly (PASM) programming. The overall task you will pursue in the book is to implement a delta compression algorithm (a way to store a string of numbers in less space), first in Spin, then in PASM, and finally in C. Along the way, I talk about Test-Driven Development and will end with a chapter on hardware manipulations.

Intended Audience

It will be helpful to have some knowledge of a programming language. The intent is to help you extend the capabilities of the Propeller processor by using C and the Assembler language. If you don't know Spin but do know another programming language (C or Python, for example), you will still be able to follow along actively.

You will learn by doing, so you must purchase a Propeller board such as the QuickStart board (`https://www.parallax.com/product/40000`) so that you can run the code.

Formatting

In this book, code listings are typeset in a typewriter font: `nSamps := 1`.

To keep the bloat down, I often elide lines that have been explained earlier. I will insert an ellipsis to indicate that: ....

I leave out or ignore

Lines of code in Spin may not have a line break. When a long line listing is broken into two because of the page width, this is indicated with an arrow: (↵). You can download the code examples from GitHub (`https://github.com/Apress/propeller-programming`). Two libraries (`FullDuplexSerial4PortPlus_0v3` and `Numbers`) are used in the code. Both can be downloaded from the Propeller Object Exchange (`http://obex.parallax.com`), and for convenience I include them in the GitHub repository.

Trains

As you will discover, I like trains! But my choice of trains as an analog for the Propeller isn't entirely arbitrary. Like the Propeller, train stations have many parallel tracks with trains moving at different speeds and performing different tasks and with the need to somehow communicate between each other and with the outside world.

As with trains there is always the possibility of a crash! Gentle programmer, as in any journey, you will experience tears and heartache en route to your destination, but if you persist, there is a great reward at the end of the journey!

PART I

Introduction

CHAPTER 1

Introduction

This is a tutorial on programming the Propeller microcontroller using both the C programming language and the Propeller Assembly (PASM) language. For many years after its introduction, the Propeller could be programmed in Spin and PASM; more recently, Parallax (the company behind the Propeller) has made a C compiler available. Spin and C are high-level *interpreted* and *compiled* languages, respectively. PASM is a *low-level* language, with a one-to-one correspondence between an instruction and the Propeller's machine code.

The advantage of PASM over Spin (and to some extent C) is speed. PASM is faster than Spin by almost two orders of magnitude, and it is faster than C by a factor of about two to five. The disadvantage of PASM is that it is cryptic and has fewer helpful shortcuts. A common task such as a loop is a single statement in C or Spin but requires more effort in PASM. Furthermore, Spin and C are well-documented, and there are a number of books and tutorials available. To learn PASM, you can turn to far fewer resources. This book is an attempt to fill that gap.

Together, we will first program a *compression/decompression* algorithm in Spin and then in PASM and finally in C and PASM. Compression refers to the process of taking a set of numbers and processing them in such a way that they can be stored in less space than they would have originally taken up. In lossless compression, those compressed numbers must still retain all the information in the original set of numbers (in lossy compression, we accept some degradation of the information in the numbers). The process of decompression is one in which those original numbers are generated

© Sridhar Anandakrishnan 2018
S. Anandakrishnan, *Propeller Programming*, https://doi.org/10.1007/978-1-4842-3354-2_1

from the compressed ones. In this book I will implement a lossless compression algorithm popular in the earthquake research community known as *delta compression* or Steim compression (named after its originator). Steim compression can reduce the space needed to store a *seismogram* (the sequence of numbers from an instrument for measuring ground motion due to an earthquake) by a factor of two or three.

We will work through the code for compression and decompression in Spin and in C. I then reproduce that code in PASM. The intent is that you should be able to follow the Spin/C code if you know some programming language. Thus, when you plunge into the PASM programming, you can focus on translating what you know from the higher-level language to the lower-level one.

If the speed of compression/decompression for the Spin/C code is fast enough to handle the sampling data rates, there may be no need to use the PASM code. For higher sampling rates, we will need to use a PASM program. Nevertheless, the Spin/C code is useful to write and run as a way to generate input for testing the PASM code.

The Propeller is most often used as an *embedded* controller to read and write electrical signals on its input and output pins. I will demonstrate these hardware interactions in all three languages as well. In this book I start with all the interaction through the terminal. Later, so that we can debug PASM code, it can be helpful to toggle a pin to see when the code enters and exits particular parts of the program. For that a logic analyzer or an oscilloscope is needed.

In the end, I find that the most convenient combination that balances simplicity of programming language and speed of operation is to use C with particular sections written in PASM.

Disclaimer   I use and enjoy programming the Propeller, but I'm by no means an expert. If you find mistakes or have suggestions for new content, I welcome corrections and improvements.

Chapters 1–4 are an introduction to the device, to the Spin language, and to Test-Driven Development. Chapters 5–10 cover the PASM programming language and hardware interactions. Chapters 11–14 cover the C language and the various modes of programming the propeller in C: pure C, so-called Cog C, and mixed C and PASM programming. I end with a chapter on using an inline assembler that injects assembly code to speed up sections of C code.

1.1 The Propeller Eight-Cog Processor

The Propeller microcontroller is a versatile and powerful device. What sets it apart from most other microcontrollers is that there are in fact eight independent, parallel, but cooperating microcontrollers (known as *cogs*) within each Propeller microcontroller. You use as many or as few cogs as you need to do the job (and can turn cogs on and off, as needed, to conserve power).

There is a wealth of information about the Propeller on the Parallax web site[1] and even more on the forums.[2]

- You will need a Propeller board (available from Parallax for $25 to $80).

- You *must* download or purchase the Propeller manual.[3]

---

[1]https://parallax.com
[2]https://goo.gl/enX7pB
[3]https://www.parallax.com/downloads/propeller-manual

- Also take a look at the Q&A.[4]

- There are detailed tutorials and getting-started guides at the web site at `http://learn.parallax.com`.

An Opinionated Aside   The Propeller is of remarkable (unique?) design because of the eight parallel *cogs*, or processors. Embedded systems (programmable controllers that are often "hidden" from users but interact with the physical world through electrical signals) require careful attention to detail when it's possible for more than one signal to arrive at nearly the same time. That worry about timing doesn't go away with the Propeller, but it is much alleviated by having eight *truly* parallel processors that can monitor and respond to events independently of each other.

The other remarkable aspect of the device is that it is useful (and used) by folks in the hobby/maker/education community as well as in commercial products.

Finally, the Propeller community is fantastically helpful. Ask questions (any question, no matter how basic) on the forums, and beginners will get a friendly welcome and gentle nudge in the right direction; those with more advanced questions sometimes get a complete, tested solution!

1.1.1 Cogs

A *cog* is a microprocessor (one of eight within the Propeller that can be individually activated and deactivated by other cogs). You provide a cog with a set of instructions and an order in which to execute those

---

[4]`https://www.parallax.com/propeller/qna/`

instructions. The cogs run in *parallel,* meaning that all the active cogs respond to each clock cycle in parallel (more on this later). A program always starts on one cog known as the *main cog.* The main cog can selectively start and stop up to seven other cogs that can independently perform tasks. All the cogs have access to all the input and output lines of the Propeller.

The Propeller as a whole can run at a variety of clock speeds depending on the needs of the program and the desire for reducing power consumption (slower speeds and fewer cogs consume less power, unsurprisingly).

Each of the eight cogs of the Propeller can operate at approximately 20 million instructions per second (MIPS) . And because the cogs run on *separate pieces of hardware,* the total capacity of the Propeller is something closer to 160MIPS.

- Each cog has access to all 32 input/output pins of the Propeller. Each cog has access to an internal counter that increments once per clock cycle and to two programmable counters that can be associated with pins.

- Each cog has access to a 32 kilobytes (KB) shared memory area called the *hub.*

- The propeller runs a Spin interpreter that converts Spin code (stored in the hub) to PASM instructions that are then copied to a cog and run there.

- Alternatively, each cog can be programmed directly in PASM; a PASM program consists of a few hundred *instructions.*

- Each cog has 2KB of internal memory for storing instructions and data.

PASM instructions fall into a few families.

- Assignment, addition, and subtraction.

- Bitwise logical operations (AND, OR, and so on).

- Bit manipulations (shift or rotate longs by a certain number of bits).

- Hub memory access (reading and writing to the hub).

- Waiting for a condition to be met (e.g., waiting for the counter to equal a value, waiting for a pin to equal a state).

- Changing the location where execution will continue (jumping to an address); without an explicit jump, the next instruction in memory is executed.

- Setting or clearing a shared lock in an atomic fashion.

- Starting and stopping cogs.

- Conditional execution of an instruction based on the value of two special flags, Z and C.

- Setting the Z and C flags. Many of the instructions mentioned can and do change these flags precisely for use by the conditional execution step.

In Figure 1-1, you can see the effect of clock speed on current consumption. The Propeller can dynamically change clock speed, so you could, for example, run at a slow speed (low power) while waiting for an event and then switch to a higher speed to process data.

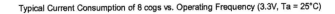

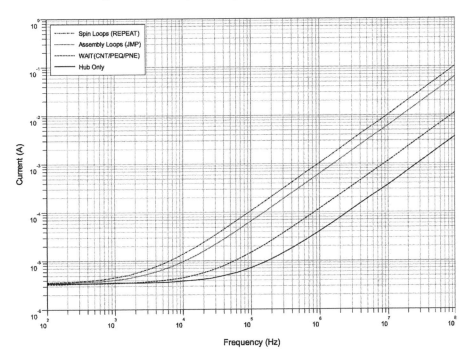

Figure 1-1. *Current consumption for eight cogs under different conditions. Horizontal axis is frequency from 100Hz to 100MHz, and vertical axis is current from 1μA to 1A. Source: Propeller P8X32A Datasheet, Parallax Semiconductor, 2011.*

1.1.2 Hubs and Cogs

The *hub* serves as a common area with 32KB of storage (versus 2KB in each cog). Each cog keeps immediately needed instructions and data internally but can request other data and instructions from the hub as needed. The key difference between cog memory and hub memory is latency. Cog memory is available instantly; hub memory operates on a round-robin basis. Each of the eight cogs is given a window of access to the hub, and if a cog misses that window, it must wait until the hub "rotates back" to it (Figure 1-2).

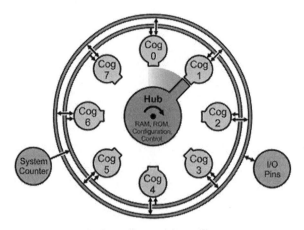

Hub and Cog Interaction

Figure 1-2. *The relationship between the hub and cogs. The hub rotates to the next cog every four clock cycles, and at that time, the cog can exchange data with the hub. Source: Propeller P8X32A Datasheet, Parallax Semiconductor, 2011.*

Initially only one cog is running. You can start up a second cog, which will run at the same clock speed and in parallel to the first cog. In other words, both cogs will execute their own instructions at *exactly the same time.* This is particularly valuable in cases where timing is critical or in cases where you need to read data from a pin at high speed (or, more likely, if you need to do both things at once).

For example, let's say we want to monitor the pulse-per-second (PPS) line from a GPS receiver[5] to synchronize the internal clock to an absolute time standard. At the same time, we may be reading data from a digitizer at rates of 100 kilobits per second (Kbps). This is 100,000 bits per second or approximately every $10\mu s$. One way to structure this program would be to have two cogs running in parallel where the first does nothing but wait for the PPS line to rise and to set the clock when it does; the second cog could be independently reading the data line.

---

[5]GPS receivers are some of the most accurate clocks in existence. Even an inexpensive GPS receiver has time accuracy of a few tens of nanoseconds.

The only time that the cogs are not completely independent is when they want to access hub resources. For example, if a cog wants to write data to hub memory, it waits its turn. The hub operates in round-robin fashion and gives each of the eight cogs its window of opportunity to write to the hub (Figure 1-2 shows a railroad turntable that is analogous: the different locomotives can access the central hub only when it's their turn).

Multi-core vs. single-core processors   To be fair, everything you will do with a Propeller microcontroller can be done with a single-processor machine. A single-processor machine—even a relatively simple one—can easily keep up with a 100Kbps data stream. These processors may have a counter module that could be set to be triggered by the PPS line, so you could synchronize to GPS time, or they may be capable of setting the PPS line as a hardware interrupt that will call a synchronization subroutine when the PPS signal arrives.

There are proponents of the Propeller, and there are those who like other processors. What I find appealing about the Propeller is the elegance of separating functionally different tasks into different cogs.

1.2 Memory Layout

We will be doing lots of messing about with memory locations and whether a number is a byte or a long, and so on, so this section is a quick high-level introduction to what the Propeller "looks like" on the inside. There are two areas of memory that we will be dealing with. One is *hub memory*. This is a 32KB area of shared space where program instructions and variables, as well as special-purpose registers, are saved. We will mainly be focusing on variables' storage and access to some of those special registers.

In the propeller, memory is addressed by byte, word (two bytes), or long (4 bytes). In hub memory, one can use all three of these memory types, but in a cog, only bytes and longs are allowed.

11

The other area of memory is *cog memory*. There are seven such areas available (the eighth, cog 0, is generally not programmed by us in PASM). PASM instructions are placed in that space, as well as storage for any variables used by that cog. It is important to keep in mind that this space is completely separate from the hub memory (and from the cog memory for other cogs). If you want to interact with the other cogs, you must do so by writing to and reading from hub memory. We will spend some time looking at that. Figure 1-3 shows a railroad turntable. The engines are stored on the spokes of the turntable and the central hub rotates to access them as needed, in similar fashion to the Propeller.

Figure 1-3. *A railroad turntable. To store locomotives in a yard and to access them at any time, the central turntable would rotate to a particular set of tracks; the locomotive would drive onto the turntable, and then the turntable would rotate to another set of tracks (or would rotate 180 degrees to reverse the direction of locomotive). Source: Photograph by Jeroen Komen.* `https://goo.gl/PjJhgZ`. *Distributed under the Creative Commons License CC-BY-SA 2.0.*

1.2.1 Hub Memory

All memory is addressed by byte. Listing 1-1 shows how memory is declared (reserved), and Figure 1-4 shows how the bytes are organized. The upper part of the code (before the DAT) is Spin code, which reserves space in hub memory; the part after the DAT is PASM code, which affects memory in a cog after a cognew command. (In this and subsequent code listings, an ellipsis [...] stands in for other lines of code that I'm not showing.)

Listing 1-1. Variable Declarations in Spin

```
1   ...
2   VAR
3     byte packBuf [8]
4     long nSamps, sampsBuf [2]
5
6   PUB MAIN
7     packBuf[0] := $00 ' not really necessary
8     packBuf[1] := $00
9     packBuf[2] := $00
10    packBuf[3] := $00
11    nSamps := $02
12    sampsBuf[0] := $00_14_00_72
13    sampsBuf[1] := $00_00_01_5c
14    cognew(@PROG, 0)
15  ...
16
17  DAT
18  PROG ORG 0
19  ...
```

```
20  :loop
21  ...
22  _ns res 1
23  _nsPtr res 1
24  FIT 496
```

All memory is addressed by byte (in both hub and cog memory).

The variables declared as byte values (packBuf[i]) are stored in consecutive memory locations.

However, the variables declared as long values (nsamps, sampsBuf[i]) are stored at every fourth memory location (because they take up four bytes each): 0x54, 0x58, and 0x5C.

The order of memory storage follows the order of how the variables are declared in the VAR section. In other words, because I declared nSamps first and then sampsBuf immediately after, that is how the memory will look.[6]

1.2.2 Cog Memory

The cog memory is also addressed by byte, but unlike in hub memory, there is no provision to reserve byte-wide memory. Everything is stored in full longs. If you want to address a byte, you have to first address a long and then mask the eight bits corresponding to the byte of interest. Each cog has 512 longs of space (2KB), of which 496 are available to the user. The last 16 longs of cog memory are reserved for special registers (PAR, OUTA, etc.).

You put PASM instructions at address zero, and the Propeller will execute that instruction and then step to the next instruction at the next location (1 long higher), and so on. An instruction is simply a 32-bit number (a very special number where every bit is important and tells

---

[6]Don't interleave byte and long declarations in VAR. The Spin compiler will store all longs first, then all words, and then all byte variables, even if you declare a byte variable before a long.

the Propeller to do something particular—add these numbers, copy this number there, etc.—but just a number nevertheless), which means that if execution accidentally wandered into areas where you have variables stored, the cog will try to execute those as if they were instructions.

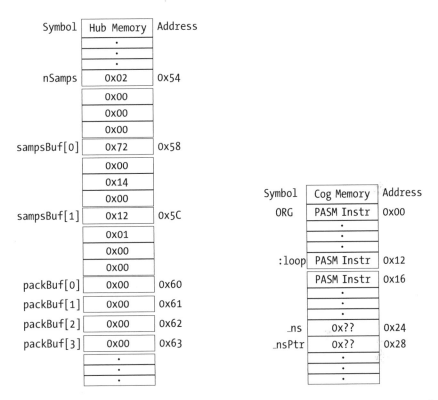

Figure 1-4. *Hub and cog memory layout from Listing 1-1. Note that memory addresses increase downward.*

1.3 Layout of This Book

In Chapter 2 I describe the underlying process of delta compression (or Steim compression). In Chapter 3 I introduce the Spin language and provide templates for a Spin program and a PASM "Hello, World" program. Here you can verify that your hardware setup is working (you *did* buy a Propeller board to run your code on, right?). In Chapter 4, I introduce a simplified version of Test-Driven Development (TDD), which I use in this book. In Chapter 5, I implement the Steim compression and decompression algorithm in Spin and verify that it is working using TDD.

Chapter 6 introduces PASM, and we begin the development of Steim compression code in PASM. In Chapter 7, I introduce methods for reading and setting pins. I implement a Serial Peripheral Interface (SPI) bus in Spin and in PASM and use that bus between two cogs (one running the main Spin code and one running the Steim PASM code). Next, I introduce semaphores (or locks) and end with examples of some useful routines in Spin: multiplication, division, loops, branching.

In Chapters 8 and 9 I continue the PASM compression algorithm development using TDD. In Chapter 10, I implement the Steim decompression routines in PASM, including TDD. Chapter 11 is devoted to some simple debugging methods for PASM code.

The last section of the book is devoted to using C to perform many of the same tasks. Chapter 12 introduces C and, in particular, the Propeller-specific peculiarities we will encounter; here we program the Steim compression routine in C. In Chapter 13 I describe *Cog-C* mode where the compression C code is launched in a new cog. In Chapter 14, I do the same but with a mix of C and PASM.

Finally, in Chapters 15 and 16, I go over the methods for interacting with hardware again, but this time in C.

CHAPTER 2

Steim Compression

Consider a freight train carrying goods—some big and some small—across the country. Rather than put each item in its own railroad car, the little things are combined and put in one car and then separated at the far end. Compression does much the same thing. Given a set of numbers (some small and some large), you squeeze the small ones together for storage and then take them apart when you need to use them.

This book is built around implementing a *delta compression* routine. Given a set of N numbers, S_i, $i = 0, ..., N - 1$, the Steim compression method is to form a set of backward differences: $\delta_j = S_j - S_{j-1}, j = 1, ..., N - 1$.[1]

These differences (along with S_0, the first sample) are packed into a compressed string, where each difference may take up less space than the original sample. To uncompress the data, each difference must have an associated code c_i indicating how many bytes were used for storing the difference: c_i, $i = 0, ..., N - 1$.

---

[1]This technique was popularized by Dr. JM Steim and has been implemented by the International Federation of Digital Seismograph Networks. The best description is in the SEED Reference Manual, "Standards for the Exchange of Earthquake Data," `https://www.fdsn.org/seed_manual/SEEDManual_V2.4.pdf`. There is no published reference to Dr. Steim's work.

© Sridhar Anandakrishnan 2018
S. Anandakrishnan, *Propeller Programming*, https://doi.org/10.1007/978-1-4842-3354-2_2

In this compression routine, the allowed sizes are 32 bits (4 bytes, or a long in Spin), 24 bits (3 bytes), 16 bits (2 bytes, or a word), and 8 bits (a byte). In more advanced compressors, 4-bit and 12-bit word lengths are allowed. I will leave that as an exercise for you!

2.1 Packing and Compressing Data

You can picture the memory impact of the compression with an example of four samples (7, 42, -12, 350) that must be compressed. Figure 2-1 shows the memory layout for these samples in panel (a) (from here out I will generally represent numbers in hexadecimal format and indicate that by prepending the number with 0x). In panel (b) I show the compressed and packed buffer layout with the 3-byte sample 0 storage and the subsequent differences stored. In panel (c) I show the compression coding.

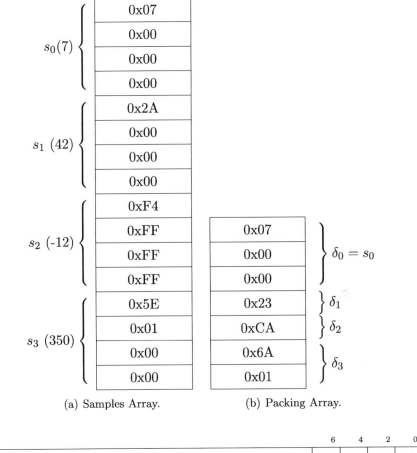

(a) Samples Array.   (b) Packing Array.

(c) Compression coding

Figure 2-1. *Compression: (a) Samples are 4 bytes long but are packed into 1–3 bytes of differences of samples. (I know a priori that my numbers always fit in 3 bytes). (b) Sample 0 is stored as is; the difference between samples 1 and 0 is stored in the smallest number of bytes possible, and so on. (c) The length of storage is itself saved in the compression code array.*

It should be apparent that this compression method is best suited for time-series data where the mean of the numbers may be large but the standard deviation is small. Steim compression is most commonly used in data from seismographs (instruments that measure the ground motion to detect earthquakes). For much of the time, the seismographs are recording background noise, which has a small sample-to-sample variability. When an earthquake occurs, however, the seismograph output can and does change dramatically from one sample to the next. Figure 2-2 shows an example of a set of seismograms after a massive and destructive earthquake in Japan. All these data needs to be recorded and stored without any loss.

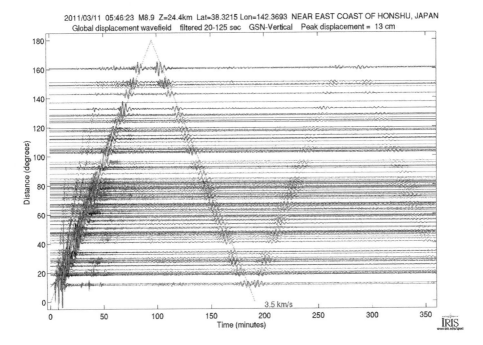

2011/03/11 05:46:23 M8.9 Z=24.4km Lat=38.3215 Lon=142.3693 NEAR EAST COAST OF HONSHU, JAPAN
Global displacement wavefield   filtered 20-125 sec   GSN-Vertical   Peak displacement = 13 cm

Figure 2-2. *Seismograms from around the world after the devastating Tohoku earthquake of March 2011 (magnitude 9). The lines show ground displacement at various seismographs ranging in distance from close to Japan (angular distance of 0 degrees) to the other side of the world from Japan (angular distance of 180 degrees). The horizontal axis is time after the earthquake occurs (in minutes). You can see the surface wave train travel around the world, back to Japan, and then repeat! In fact, the earth "rung like a bell" for hours after this event. Source:* `http://ds.iris.edu/ds/nodes/dmc/specia levents/2011/03/11/tohoku-japan-earthquake/`.

2.2 Specification

Input numbers must be valid 32-bit numbers, but the *dynamic range* of the samples is limited to 24 bits (that is the limit of our digitizer). Therefore, every sample can be represented and stored in at most 3 bytes. However, most programming languages prefer 4-byte numbers. Thus, on

21

decompression, numbers should be 4 bytes long, with the uppermost byte *sign extended* from bit 23 (more on this later).

In the main cog, I will define the following:

- nsamps: A long variable holding the number of samples *N* to process.

- sampsBuf: A long array holding the samples s_i.

- packBuf: A byte array holding the compressed and packed differences δ_i.

- codeBuf: A long array holding the compression code for each compressed sample.

- nCompr: A long variable holding the populated number of bytes in packBuf.

Here is what happens:

1. The compression program will compress nsamps numbers from the sampsBuf array and populate the output variables packBuf, codeBuf, and nCompr.

2. If nsamps is greater than the length of sampsBuf, return an error by setting ncompr to -1.

3. For sample zero:

   - STEIM SHALL compress the first sample, s_0, by storing its bits 0 to 23 (the lower 3 bytes) into packBuf.

   - STEIM SHALL store CODE24 in the lowest 2 bits of codeBuf.

   - STEIM SHALL set nCompr to 3.

     (My digitizer has a 24-bit dynamic range, so all numbers fit within 3 or fewer bytes.)

4. For sample j $(0 < j < N)$:

    •   STEIM will form the backward difference $\delta_j = s_j - s_{j-1}$
        and determine whether the difference would fit
        completely within 1, 2, or 3 bytes and SHALL append
        those bytes to packBuf.

    •   STEIM SHALL increment nCompr by 1, 2, 3,
        according as the number of bytes needed for δ_j.

    •   STEIM SHALL place the appropriate code (CODE08,
        CODE16, or CODE24) in comprBuf.

5. Finally, the decompression routine takes as input
    nsamps, packBuf, codeBuf, and nCompr and SHALL
    populate sampsBuf correctly.

2.3 Implementation

Now that we have a concise specification for the procedure, we will
implement it in the following chapters (first in Spin, then in PASM,
then in C, and finally in C and PASM). The way we will build up the
implementations is similar in all cases. We will write a test for each of the
previous bullets, and then we will write the code so that it passes the test.

CHAPTER 3

Introduction to Spin

Let's set up a Spin and PASM template and make sure you can compile the Spin and PASM program, that you can connect to the Propeller and download the binary file, and that you can see the output.

A few notes: Spin is sensitive to indentation (PASM is not). Comments begin with a single quote (') and continue for the remainder of the line. Block comments are delineated by curly braces ({ and }).

In general, strive for simplicity and clarity in the code when starting out (even at the expense of speed). Once the code is working, you can tweak portions to speed them up if you need better performance.

Neither Spin nor PASM is sensitive to case. Nevertheless, we will hold to these conventions:

- All caps are used for block identifiers (CON, OBJ, VAR, PUB, PRI, and DAT), constants, and function names (also called method names).

- Words in function names are separated by underscores (_).

- Variable names use lowercase and "camel case" (capitalized second and later words, for example, sampsPerSecond).

- An underscore is used as the first letter of variables in PASM code.

- A lowercase p is used as the first letter of array address variable names ("pointers") in functions.

© Sridhar Anandakrishnan 2018
S. Anandakrishnan, *Propeller Programming*, https://doi.org/10.1007/978-1-4842-3354-2_3

Finally, Spin has a flexible and friendly way of representing numbers. Prepend $ (dollar sign) for hexadecimal numbers and % (percent sign) for binary; numbers without a preceding symbol are decimal numbers. You can insert underscores anywhere in a number, and they are ignored by the compiler. They are syntactic "sugar" to help reduce errors—particularly with binary numbers with long strings of ones and zeros. So, you can say this:

```
1  pi4 := 3 _1415 ' the _ is ignored pi4 =31415
2  pi4 := $7A_B7
3  pi4 := %0111 _1010_1011_0111
```

BINARY AND DECIMAL AND HEX, OH MY

The Propeller (and computers in general) store numbers in *binary* format.

- In a *decimal* representation of a number (what we are used to in real life), digits can range from 0 to 9, and a number like 42 is read as "2 times 1 plus 4 times 10."

- In a *binary* representation, only the digits 0 and 1 are allowed, and the number 42 is represented as 101010, which is read as (right to left) "0 times 1 plus 1 times 2 plus 0 times 4 plus 1 times 8 plus 0 times 16 plus 1 times 32" (32 + 8 + 2 = 42).

- In a *hexadecimal* (or hex) representation, digits range from 0 to 9 and A to F (where *A* is 10, *B* is 11, up to *F*, which is 15). The number 42 is represented as 2A, which is read as "A, which is 10, times 1 plus 2 times 16" (32 + 10 = 42).

In this book (and many computer books), a hex number is written as 0x2A (the 0x signals that the number should be interpreted as a hex number). However, in a Spin or PASM program, that would be written as $2A. In a C program, that would be written as 0x2A.

In this book and in C, a binary number is written as 0b00101010. In Spin and PASM, it is written as %0010_1010.

Yes, I know, it would be nice if we could all agree to use the same vocabulary, but what a boring world that would be!

```
1   theAnswerDec := 42          ' decimal 42
2   theAnswerHex := $2A         ' hexadecimal 0x2A
3   theAnswerBin := %00101010 ' binary 0 b00101010.
```

By convention, we show only as many decimal numbers as needed, so for example for the number 7, we don't say 007, just 7. However, also by convention we always show hex numbers in groups of two, so we would write that as $07 or 0x07, and in binary we show groups of eight: %0000_0111 or 0b00000111.

There are 8 binary digits per byte and 2 bytes per word (16 bits) and 4 bytes per long (32 bits). A byte is a collection of 8 bits. A byte can contain *unsigned* numbers from 0 to 255; a word can contain numbers from 0 to 65,535; and a long can contain numbers from 0 to 4,294,967,295 (about 4 billion).

The advantage of a hex representation is that each *byte* (a collection of 8 bits) can be succinctly *and naturally* written as two hex digits. The largest number that can be written in 8 bits is the number you and I know in decimal as 255 (5 times 1 plus 5 times 10 plus 2 times 100) or binary *11111111* (I won't write out the sums here, but you should). In hex, that number is *FF* (15 times 1 plus 15 times 16). There are many advantages to this method of writing numbers and many resources on the Web for understanding it.

One enormously useful tool is a calculator app that has a "programmer's mode" that can show numbers in the different *bases* (bases are the underlying number system, either binary, decimal, or hex).

3.1 Negative Numbers

If we decide that an eight-bit number is *unsigned*, then it can store numbers from 0 to 255 (%0000_0000 to %1111_1111: 1 times 1 plus 1 times 2 plus 1 times 4, etc., up to 1 times 128 = 255).

However, if we decide that an 8-bit number is *signed*, then it can store numbers from -128 to 127. The most significant bit is referred to as the *sign bit*, and if it is 1, then the number is a negative number. Thus, the same set of bits (e.g., i =%1111_1111) would be i = 255 if i were signed, and it would be i = –1 if i were unsigned.

Negative numbers are stored in a "two's-complement" representation.[1] You don't need to worry about the details of what that means, except to be careful when changing the size of storage from, for example, 8 bits to 32 bits. Now that we have "laid the rails" for our work (Figure 3-1 shows some actual rails!), let's look at how the propeller implements memory.

---

[1]See the Wikipedia page at https://en.wikipedia.org/wiki/Two%27s_complement for more information.

Figure 3-1. *A crew of railroad workers poses for the camera in 1911. Photographer unknown. In Nelson, Scott Reynolds (2007), Ain't Nothing but a Man: My Quest to Find the Real John Henry, National Geographic Books, ISBN: 9781426300004.* https://upload. wikimedia.org/wikipedia/commons/5/51/A_crew_of_railroad_ workers_poses_for_the_camera_in_1911.jpg. *Wikimedia Commons, no license attached.*

3.2 Memory Layout

Absolute memory addresses increase from zero, incrementing by one for each byte. There are three storage lengths in the propeller: bytes, words (2 bytes), and longs (4 bytes).

Propellers are *little-endian* devices. Thus, the lowest byte of a long number is stored at a lower memory location than the higher bytes in that number. (Note that the Propeller happily allows you to modify *any* memory location!)

3.3 Spin Template

Let's start with the Spin file. Listing 3-1 is a template that you can use to make sure your Propeller is working and connected and that the compiler and loader on your computer are working. There are a couple of options for the computer side. Parallax supports an excellent Propeller Tool[2] (Windows only), and there is a cross-platform PropellerIDE tool[3] (both of which have a compiler, program loader, and serial terminal included). I use separate command-line tools for compiling the code (`openspin`) and loading the Propeller (`propeller-load`), which are included with the PropellerIDE package.

The Propeller Tool and the PropellerIDE tool both include an editor that colorizes the code and handles indentation properly. You can also use a stand-alone text editor (such as Atom, emacs, and vi) and use command-line tools.

3.3.1 Hello, World

Trust Me, It's Good for You!   I know this seems silly, but instead of downloading this file from GitHub or cutting and pasting this from the screen, *type in the whole file by hand!* It may seem like a waste of time, but I guarantee you that in the process of finding bugs and fixing them, you will learn way more than you can imagine.

---

[2]https://www.parallax.com/downloads/propeller-tool-software-windows-spin-assembly

[3]https://www.parallax.com/downloads/propeller-p8x32a-software

Listing 3-1. Spin Program Template for "Hello, World"

```
1   {*
2    * Spin Template - curly braces are block comments
3    *}
4   ' single quotes are line comments
5   CON ' Clock mode settings
6     _CLKMODE = XTAL1 + PLL16X
7     _XINFREQ = 5_000_000
8
9     ' system freq as a constant
10    FULL_SPEED  = (( _clkmode - xtal1) >> 6) * _xinfreq
11    ' ticks in 1ms
12    ONE_MS      = FULL_SPEED / 1_000
13    ' ticks in 1us
14    ONE_US      = FULL_SPEED / 1_000_000
15
16  CON ' Pin map
17
18    DEBUG_TX_TO   = 30
19    DEBUG_RX_FROM = 31
20
21  CON ' UART ports
22    DEBUG             =        0
23    DEBUG_BAUD        = 115200
24
25    UART_SIZE         =      100
26    CR                =       13
27    LF                =       10
28    SPACE             =       32
29    TAB               =        9
```

```
30    COLON               =      58
31    COMMA               =      44
32
33  OBJ
34    UARTS : " FullDuplexSerial4portPlus_0v3 " ' 1 COG for 3 ↵
      serial ports
35    NUM : " Numbers " ' Object for writing numbers to debug
36
37  VAR
38    byte mainCogId, serialCogId
39
40  PUB MAIN
41
42    mainCogId := cogid
43    LAUNCH_SERIAL_COG
44    PAUSE_MS(500)
45
46    UARTS.STR(DEBUG, string (CR, LF, " mainCogId : "))
47    UARTS.DEC(DEBUG, mainCogId)
48    UARTS.STR(DEBUG, string (CR, LF, "Hello, World !", ↵
      CR, LF))
49    repeat
50      PAUSE_MS(1000)
51
52  PUB LAUNCH_SERIAL_COG
53  " method that sets up the serial ports
54    NUM.INIT
55    UARTS.INIT
56    ' Add DEBUG port
57    UARTS.ADDPORT(DEBUG, DEBUG_RX_FROM, DEBUG_TX_TO, ↵
      -1, -1, 0, %000000, DEBUG_BAUD)
```

```
58    UARTS.START
59    serialCogId := UARTS.GETCOGID
60    ' Start the ports
61    PAUSE_MS(300)
62
63  PUB PAUSE_MS(mS)
64    waitcnt(clkfreq /1000 * mS + cnt)
65
66  ' Program ends here
```

- **Lines 1–4**: Comments.

- **Lines 5–31**: Constants (CON) blocks. They are separated into individual blocks solely for purposes of organization.

- **Lines 33–37**: Objects (OBJ) block. The compiler will read the files named in quotes to the right of the colon (after appending .spin to the name) and assign constants and methods to the symbol to the left of the colon. So, all functions in Numbers.spin are available as NUM.FUNCTION_NAME. A function is a block of code that can be called, possibly with arguments (you will sometimes see them referred to as *methods*).

- **Lines 39–40**: Variables declaration block VAR. Variables declared here are initialized to zero. The size of memory is determined by the variable type (byte, word, or long).

- **Lines 42–50**: The first function in the top-level (or entry) file is executed by the Spin compiler in cog 0. By convention, we call it MAIN.

- **Lines 52–65**: Functions that can be called by MAIN.

The first CON block is the declaration of a set of constants for the Propeller clock. For now, simply copy the lines. I'll come back to what they mean later. The second and third blocks are constants for the serial port. In constant blocks, the constant name and value are separated by an equal sign (=). Later in the code, assignment to variables is done using :=.

The next block (OBJ) is like #include in C; it's a way to bring in external libraries. The desired name for the library and the string containing the file name of the library (without the .spin extension) are separated by a colon.

```
LIBNAME : "LibFile" ' read in file LibFile.spin and assign it
to LIBNAME
```

From now on you can refer to the functions and constants in that library by invoking this:

```
LIBNAME.LIBFUNCTION to call a function or method LIBFUNCTION in
library LIBNAME and LIBNAME#LIBCONSTANT to refer to a constant
LIBCONSTANT defined in that library[4].
```

The next block is a VAR where variables are declared and initialized to zero.

Finally, the actual program begins at the first PUB method (named MAIN by convention). This block is run automatically after the program is loaded on the Propeller. This is the "entry point" into the program (like int main() in C). From within MAIN you can call functions with any required arguments in parentheses. If there are no arguments, there is no need for the parentheses.

In the template some of the function calls are part of Spin (cogid, for example), some are written by us (PAUSE_MS), and some are part of an

---

[4]The two libraries are available on the Propeller Object Exchange (obex. parallax.com) or in the GitHub repo (https://github.com/sanandak/ propbook-code).

object or library (UARTS.STR). Functions may return a value (for example, cogid does), which we can assign to a variable using := (a colon followed by the equal sign).

3.3.2 Running the Program

If you have openspin and propeller-load (or propman) on your path (Linux and macOS),[5] the following are the commands to run from a terminal.

The following will create a .binary file:

```
$ openspin ./spin_template.spin
```

The following command will send it to the Propeller. Your serial port number will differ. The propeller-load program is invoked with the -r and -t flags that instruct the Propeller to run the program after it is downloaded and to start a terminal to view messages from the Propeller, respectively.

```
$ propeller-load -p /dev/cu.usbserial-A103FFE0 \
                -t -r spin_template.binary
Propeller Version 1 on /dev/cu.usbserial-A103FFE0
Loading spin_template.binary to hub memory
3924 bytes sent
Verifying RAM ... OK
[Entering terminal mode. Type ESC or Control-C to exit.]
mainCogId:    0
Hello, World!
```

---

[5]Using sh or bash on a Mac, the command is as follows: export PATH=/ Applications/PropellerIDE.app/Contents/MacOS/:$PATH. On Linux, the command is as follows: export PATH=/opt/parallax/bin:$PATH.

Alternatively, you can use the PropellerIDE shown in Figure 3-2.[6]

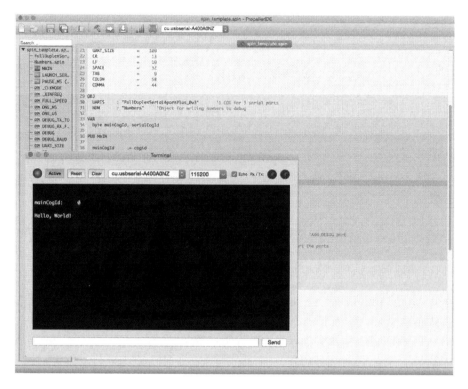

Figure 3-2. *Main window and terminal window for PropellerIDE*

Congratulations! You have successfully seen that the Propeller is attached, that you can communicate with it, that the clock is set correctly, and that you can compile and download a program and view the output. That's a lot!

---

[6]https://www.parallax.com/downloads/propelleride-software-mac

3.4 PASM Template

Let's add a minimal PASM cog called HELLO. Here we will include the code for the new cog at the end of the template.spin file (copy the template to helloO.spin). Later, when we start working on the real code, we will put the Spin and PASM code in their own files. The main changes in the file are shown in Listing 3-2.

Listing 3-2. Changes to spin template.spin to Include PASM Cog Code (ch3/pasm template.spin)

```
1  ...
2  ' in VAR
3    byte helloCogId
4
5  ...
6  ' in MAIN
7    helloCogId := -1
8    helloCogId := cognew(@HELLO, 0)
9
10   UARTS.STR(DEBUG, string (CR, LF, " helloCogId : "))
11   UARTS.DEC(DEBUG, helloCogId)
12   UARTS.PUTC(DEBUG, CR)
13   UARTS.PUTC(DEBUG, LF)
14 ...
15
16 ' in a new DAT section at end
17 DAT ' pasm cog HELLO
18   HELLO ORG 0
19
20 :mainLoop
```

```
21      jmp #:mainLoop
22
23      FIT 496
```

This PASM code is the text between the DAT block marker and the FIT 496 instruction. This program does very little; it just runs an infinite loop (the jmp command jumps to the line labeled :mainLoop, which brings it right back to the jmp...).

The structure of the files and cogs is as follows. The file helloO.spin has the MAIN method, as well as a DAT section where the PASM program HELLO is defined. The file FullDuplexSerial has a Spin part where the methods DEC, HEX, PUTC, and so on, are defined, as well as a DAT part for the PASM code. Finally, the Numbers.spin file has only Spin code.

However the "cog view" of the Propeller is more like the following. The MAIN method calls a UARTS method (in the FullDuplexSerial file/object) named UARTS.START. This method includes a call to cognew that starts a new cog that manipulates the serial port lines with the correct timing. In addition, the MAIN method itself calls cognew. Each cognew command launches a new cog with code that is in the appropriate DAT section. At the end of the MAIN method, the cogs are as follows:

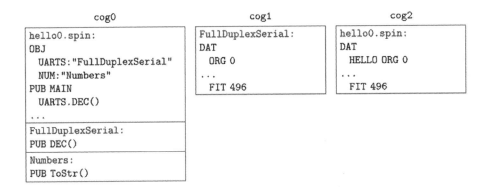

So, for example, when MAIN calls the method UARTS.DEC(), that code runs in cog 0, but it passes instructions to cog 1 that does the actual hardware manipulations of the serial line.

Cog 0 isn't a special cog. When the Propeller boots, it loads a Spin *interpreter* into cog 0 that reads, interprets, and executes Spin code (code that is stored in hub memory). You can launch a second cog that also has a Spin interpreter, but in this tutorial, we will load PASM code into those new cogs.

Now run this (along with print statements to print out the serial and hello cog IDs):

```
% propman  -t  hello0.binary
pm.loader: [cu.usbserial-A400AONZ] Preparing  image...
pm.loader: [cu.usbserial-A400AONZ] Downloading to RAM...
pm.loader: [cu.usbserial-A400AONZ] Verifying  RAM...
pm.loader: [cu.usbserial-A400AONZ] Success!
Entering terminal on cu.usbserial-A400AONZ
```

```
Press Ctrl+C to exit
--------------------------------------
mainCogId:         0
Hello, World
serialCogId:       1
helloCogId:        2
```

(In this case I used the propman command instead of propeller-load.) Congratulations again! You have started a PASM cog successfully.

3.5 Template for PASM Code in a Separate File

Unless your PASM code is very simple, you will want to move that code to a separate file. This will allow you to turn that functionality into an *object* that can be included in any project.

Edit hello0.spin and create two files: hello_Demo.spin and hello_pasm.spin. The file hello_Demo is derived from hello0 with the changes shown in Listing 3-3.

Listing 3-3. Changes to pasm template.spin When PASM Code Is in a Separate File (ch3/hello Demo.spin and ch3/hello pasm.spin)

```
1  ...
2  OBJ
3    ... ' add this
4    HELLO: " hello_pasm " 'pasm cog is in a different file
5
6  PUB MAIN
7  ...
8
9    helloCogId := -1
```

```
10    ' replace cognew (@HELLO, 0) with the following 2 lines
11    HELLO.INIT
12    helloCogId:= HELLO.START
13
14    ' HELLO.STOP would stop the cog
15    ...
16  ' delete the DAT section
```

The line in the OBJ section will include the hello_pasm code as HELLO. Next, instead of calling cognew directly, you initialize and start the cog by calling functions in the library HELLO. The HELLO.START method will return the number of the newly launched cog.

Create a new file called hello_pasm.spin and type in the code in Listing 3-4.

Listing 3-4. Contents of hello_pasm.spin

```
 1  {*
 2   * pasm template for code in a separate file from main
 3   *}
 4
 5  VAR
 6    byte ccogid
 7
 8  PUB INIT
 9    ccogid := -1
10
11  PUB START
12    STOP
13    ccogid:=cognew(@HELLO, 0)
14    return ccogid
15
16  PUB STOP
```

```
17    if ccogid <> -1
18       cogstop(ccogid)
19       ccogid:= -1
20
21 DAT ' pasm cog HELLO
22 HELLO ORG 0
23
24 : mainLoop
25    jmp #:mainLoop
26
27 FIT 496
```

- **Lines 5–6:** Declare a variable ccogid that is local to this file. ccogid is either 0–7 for a valid cog number or -1 if the cog is not running.

- **Lines 8–9:** The INIT method, well, initializes variables. In this case, you want to ensure that ccogid is set to -1 to indicate that the cog is not running (when the variable is first declared, it is set to zero, which isn't what you want).

- **Lines 11–19:** The START and STOP methods are straightforward. Start a new cog (after stopping it, in case it is already running) and return the number of the newly launched cog. To stop a cog, make sure it really is running and then stop it. Set the cog ID to -1 to indicate that it is no longer active.

3.6 Summary

In this chapter, I laid some rails for running a new PASM cog. The cog does nothing so far. Again, I want to emphasize that once you launch a cog, it is *entirely separate* from other cogs. It has access to hub memory, but if two cogs want to share information through the hub, they both need some way to know where to look. The most confusing part of programming PASM for beginners is getting information into and out of the cogs (at least it was for me!).

Shall we try to connect the cogs? Figure 3-3 is a famous photograph of the ceremony when the two halves of the US Transcontinental railroad met and one could take a train from New York to San Francisco! Take a break and continue with the next chapter when you are ready.

Figure 3-3. *Connecting the Eastern and Western halves of the Transcontinental Railroad at Promontory Summit, Utah, May 10, 1869.*

CHAPTER 4

Test-Driven Development

One of the techniques I will be using is Test-Driven Development (TDD). You don't need to use TDD, but I find it helpful as a learning aide. TDD is rapidly becoming the norm in large software projects. The advantages of this method of development are manifold. In collaborative projects, developers can ensure that their changes don't inadvertently break something elsewhere. In long-lived projects, when you return to something from a long time ago, you can study the tests to maintain the code. Even in small projects (such as this one), using TDD will give you confidence that the results are correct.

The idea behind TDD is that you write a specification of what the program is supposed to do; you then write a test for a small piece of the program. Then, and only then, write the *minimal* amount of code that lets the test pass. Then write another test and another piece of code to pass that test...and run *all* the tests every time to make sure your changes haven't broken anything. Once you have enough tests that cover the specification and all the tests pass, you are done. If you ever change the code (or the specification), then you rerun the tests.

© Sridhar Anandakrishnan 2018
S. Anandakrishnan, *Propeller Programming*, https://doi.org/10.1007/978-1-4842-3354-2_4

For example, here is my specification for a program, SQR, to square a number:

1. SQR(i) SHALL return the square of *i*, so long as the result doesn't overflow a 32-bit number.

2. The program SHALL return -1 if the square of the number would overflow.

The first test, TEST_THAT_SQR_2_IS_4, runs SQR(2) and then asks the question "Is the result 4?" The function prints OK or FAIL depending on whether the answer is TRUE or FALSE. It will also print an informational message. (The full code is on GitHub; Listing 4-1 shows the parts related to TDD.)

Listing 4-1. Spin Program to Demonstrate TDD (ch04/tdd 0.spin)

```
1   ' set up clock here - more on that later
2   ...
3
4   PUB MAIN
5
6      'Initialize the Terminal and TDD here - more on that later
7   ...
8
9      " run the tests
10     TEST_THAT_SQR_2_IS_4
11     TEST_THAT_SQR_BIG_IS_NEG1
12     TEST_THAT_SQR_NEG_BIG_IS_NEG1
13
14  PUB SQR(x)
15     return x*x
16
```

```
17  PUB TEST_THAT_SQR_2_IS_4 | t0
18    t0 := 4 == SQR (2)
19    TDD.ASSERT_TRUTHY(t0, string("Test that SQR (2) == 4"))
20
21  PUB TEST_THAT_SQR_BIG_IS_NEG1 | t0
22    t0 := -1 == SQR(1<<30)
23    TDD.ASSERT_TRUTHY(t0, string("Test that SQR(big) == -1"))
24
25  PUB TEST_THAT_SQR_NEG_BIG_IS_NEG1 | t0
26    t0 := -1 == SQR(-(1<<30))
27    TDD.ASSERT_TRUTHY(t0, string("Test that SQR(-big) == -1"))
```

- **Lines 11–13:** Calls to the testing methods.

- **Lines 15–16:** The method under test, SQR.

- **Lines 18–20:** A method to test that 2×2 == 4. t0 will be true if SQR(2) returns 4. The method TDD.ASSERT_ TRUTHY takes two arguments: t0 and a string. It prints out the string and then either OK or FAIL depending on whether t0 is true or false.

- **Lines 22–28:** Two additional tests.

TDD is simply a formal layer over what people do in an *ad hoc* manner when programming. You write your code and run it with some example inputs and verify that it works. With TDD, that process is *saved with the code* that you are developing and can (and should) be rerun every time you make changes to the code. Ideally, you are striving for 100 percent *coverage*, where the tests traverse all the lines of code that you have written by appropriately setting the inputs. By convention, the tests are simple and test a small piece of the code. By running all the tests, you hope to cover all the lines of the program under test. Also, by convention, the test names are verbose and grammatical so that they are self-documenting.

Let's run the tests. As you can see, there is a problem with the code. The tests are written to meet my specification, but the code fails some of my tests. It passes the test to square a small number but not to square a large one.

```
Propeller Version 1 on /dev/cu.usbserial - A103FFE0
Loading tdd_0 . binary to hub memory
4308 bytes sent
Verifying RAM ... OK
[Entering terminal mode. Type ESC or Control -C to exit.]

Test that SQR (2) == 4
... ok
Test that SQR(big) == -1
*** FAIL
```

The test for overflow after multiplication has failed. Let's modify SQR so that it passes those tests. Spin has two forms of multiplication. The standard from, *, will restrict the result to 32 bits. The alternative form, **, will return the upper 32 bits of the multiplication.

```
1  PUB SQR(x) | t
2    t := x ** x ' multiply and return high long
3    if t
4       return -1
5    return x*x
```

Let's rerun the tests and ensure that all the tests pass.

```
Test that SQR (2) == 4
... ok
Test that SQR(big) == -1
```

```
... ok
Test that SQR(-big) == -1
... ok
```

4.1 TDD Spin Code

The TDD Spin library is quite simple (see Listing 4-2). Define variables local to TDD (debugging port, number of tests run, etc.) and then print out the message and test result.

Listing 4-2. TDD Library (libs/TestDrivenDevelopment.spin)

```
1   { TestDrivenDevelopment .spin: Test Driven Development }
2
3   VAR
4       byte debug, nTest, nPass, nFail
5
6   OBJ
7     UARTS : " FullDuplexSerial4portPlus_Ov3 " '1 COG for 3 ↵
      serial ports
8
9   DAT
10    OK byte "... ok", 13, 10, 0
11    FAIL byte "*** FAIL", 13, 10, 0
12
13  PUB INIT(debugport)
14      debug := debugport
15      nTest := nPass := nFail := 0
16
17  PUB ASSERT_TRUTHY(condition, msg)
18      nTest++
```

```
19      UARTS.PUTC(debug, 13)
20      UARTS.PUTC(debug, 10)
21      UARTS.STR(debug, msg)
22      UARTS.PUTC(debug, 13)
23      UARTS.PUTC(debug, 10)
24      'UARTS.DEC(debug, t)
25      if condition <> 0
26        UARTS.STR(debug, @OK)
27        nPass++
28        return TRUE
29      else
30        UARTS.STR(debug, @FAIL)
31        nFail++
32        return FALSE
33
34  PUB SUMMARIZE
35    UARTS.STR(DEBUG, string(" Tests Run: "))
36    UARTS.DEC(DEBUG, nTest)
37    UARTS.PUTC(DEBUG, 13)
38    UARTS.PUTC(DEBUG, 10)
39    UARTS.STR(DEBUG, string(" Tests Passed : "))
40    UARTS.DEC(DEBUG, nPass)
41    UARTS.PUTC(DEBUG, 13)
42    UARTS.PUTC(DEBUG, 10)
43    UARTS.STR(DEBUG, string(" Tests Failed : "))
44    UARTS.DEC(DEBUG, nFail)
45    UARTS.PUTC(DEBUG, 13)
46    UARTS.PUTC(DEBUG, 10)
```

- **Lines 3–4:** Variables local to TDD that are set/reset by the INIT method.

- **Lines 9–11:** A data block in which you reserve memory for the message strings. These are used over and over again, and rather than generate them each time, you can define and declare them once. The symbol OK is a series of bytes made of the ASCII characters for ...ok and CR and LF (carriage return and line feed, respectively). The final 0 informs the printer that the string terminates here.

- **Lines 13–15:** Initialize the variables.

- **Lines 17–32:** Print out the message and either OK or FAIL. In line 26 and line 30, I pass the address of the memory space I reserved in the DAT section. UARTS.STR will print out the bytes at @OK or @FAIL up to the terminating NULL (0).

- **Lines 34–46:** Print out a summary.

4.2 Summary

In Test-Driven Development, you first write the specification. Next, you write a test to exercise one part of the specification. It will fail. So, you write the code to allow the test to pass. When it passes, you write another test and the associated code, and so on. By the end, you should have tests that fully represent the specification, and you should have code that passes all the tests. If you so much as add a comment, you rerun all the tests!

If you ever change your specification, then you write new tests to cover those changes. If you ever change the code (be it ever so trivial a change!), rerun the tests. In collaborative projects, this is particularly important. When different people submit their updated code, the tests can be run automatically, and any failed tests are immediately apparent. This is called *continuous integration* and is aimed at reducing the manual labor of merging many different workers.

Now that we have a testing framework in place, shall we plow on? Figure 4-1 shows the work needed to clear a path forward.

Figure 4-1. *Train in snowdrift, Bernina Railway, Switzerland. Source: CJ Allen, The Steel Highway, 1928.*

CHAPTER 5

Compression in Spin

In this chapter, we will implement the compressor and decompressor purely in Spin using Test-Driven Development (TDD) methods. Rather than jumping straight into a PASM implementation, starting with a Spin version lets us ease into the problem and also debug more effectively. Once we have a working algorithm in Spin, we will translate it to PASM. In addition, a Spin version can act as a simulator to produce compressed data streams that the PASM decompressor will have to successfully operate on, and vice versa.

5.1 Structure of the Project

There will be two spin files: `steim_spin0.spin` and `steim_spin0 Demo.spin`. The file `steim_spin0.spin` is where the actual compressor and decompressor are implemented as a separate object. The file `steim_spin0 Demo.spin` is the driver file with the `MAIN` entry point into the code, as well as where the testing methods are defined. In addition, ensure that the file `TestDrivenDevelopment.spin` is in the same directory. Your directory should look like this:

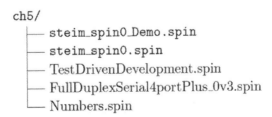

```
ch5/
    ├── steim_spin0_Demo.spin
    ├── steim_spin0.spin
    ├── TestDrivenDevelopment.spin
    ├── FullDuplexSerial4portPlus_0v3.spin
    └── Numbers.spin
```

© Sridhar Anandakrishnan 2018
S. Anandakrishnan, *Propeller Programming*, https://doi.org/10.1007/978-1-4842-3354-2_5

5.2 Goals of This Chapter

In this chapter, we will write the Steim compressor and decompressor in Spin. Remember, we have an array of long samples (4 bytes each) called sampsBuf. The compressor will produce a byte array, packBuf, which contains the packed or compressed data. We want to do the following:

- Start the process by copying 3 bytes from sampsBuf[0] to packBuf. This is done just once to initialize the compressor.

- Take the difference of sampsBuf[1] - sampsBuf[0]. If that difference fits in 1 byte, then put that 1 byte in packBuf. If that difference is 2 bytes, put those 2 bytes in packBuf, and if that difference is 3 bytes, put those 3 bytes into packBuf.

- Store a 2-bit code in comprCodeBuf that reflects which of three things we did.

- Do the previous two steps repeatedly for all the samples (Figure 5-1 shows an example of a real-world "loop").

Figure 5-1. *The Loop, Agony Point, Darjeeling Hill Railway, 1880.*
Photo uploaded by Bourne and Shepherd; artist unknown. Public
domain.

5.3 First Iteration

Begin by copying the template `spin_template.spin` and saving it as
`steim_spin0_Demo.spin`. Listing 5-1 is the *driver* program that sets up the
Propeller and then runs the tests to exercise the code. Make the changes
shown in the file.

Listing 5-1. steim_spin0_Demo: First Iteration of Implementing the Compression in Spin

```
1   OBJ
2     UARTS       : " FullDuplexSerial4portPlus_0v3 "
3     NUM         : " Numbers "
4     STEIM : " steim_spin0 "                    ' <<
5     TDD : " TestDrivenDevelopment "            ' <<
6
7   CON
8     NSAMPS_MAX = 128                           ' <<
9
10  VAR
11    byte mainCogId, serialCogId
12    byte comprCogId                            ' <<
13    byte packBuf[NSAMPS_MAX<<2]                ' <<
14
15    long nsamps, ncompr                        ' <<
16    long sampsBuf[NSAMPS_MAX]                   ' <<
17    long comprCodeBuf[NSAMPS_MAX>>4]            ' <<
18
19  PUB MAIN
20      mainCogId := cogid
21      LAUNCH_SERIAL_COG
22      PAUSE_MS(500)
23
24      UARTS.STR(DEBUG, string(CR, " Compression ", CR, LF))
25      UARTS.STR(DEBUG, string(" mainCogId: "))
26      UARTS.DEC(DEBUG, mainCogId)
27      UARTS.PUTC(DEBUG, CR)
28      UARTS.PUTC(DEBUG, LF)
```

```
29        STEIM.INIT(NSAMPS_MAX)                    ' <<
30        TDD.INIT(DEBUG)                           ' <<
31        TEST_THAT_SAMP0_IS_PROPERLY_PACKED        ' <<
32        TDD.SUMMARIZE                             ' <<
33
34   PRI TEST_THAT_SAMP0_IS_PROPERLY_PACKED | t0, nc
35        nsamps := 1
36        sampsBuf[0] := $AB_CD_EF
37        nc := STEIM.COMPRESS(@sampsBuf, nsamps, @packBuf, ↵
         @comprCodeBuf)
38        t0 := nc <> -1
39        t0 &= (packBuf[0] == sampsBuf[0] & $FF)
40        t0 &= (packBuf[1] == sampsBuf[0] >> 8 & $FF)
41        t0 &= (packBuf[2] == sampsBuf[0] >> 16 & $FF)
42        TDD.ASSERT_TRUTHY(t0, string("Test that samp0 is properly ↵
         packed"))
```

- **Lines 15–17:** Declare the arrays where the packed samples will be stored (packBuf), the samples themselves (sampsBuf), and where the compression codes will be stored (comprCodeBuf). I know that packBuf will be at most four times the length of NSAMPS_MAX and that comprCodeBuf will be 1/16th that length.

- **Lines 30–31:** Initialize the STEIM and TDD objects.

- **Lines 32–33:** Run the test and finish.

- **Lines 36–38:** Perform the compression for a single sample.

- **Lines 39–42:** Verify whether the output is as we expect.

- **Line 43:** Perform the test and print the results.

Add all the lines marked with '<< and add the method TEST_THAT_
SAMPO_IS_PROPERLY_PACKED. Lines 4–5 add the STEIM and TDD objects.
From now on, any method in the file steim_spin.spin can be called by
STEIM.METH_NAME. Similarly, any constant in that file is STEIM#CONSTANT_
NAME. Lines 13–17 declare the new variables that will be needed by the
compression and the new arrays where the uncompressed samples live
before compression (sampsBuf) and where the compressed bytes live
(packBuf).

Finally, in lines 30–31 the two objects are initialized, and in line 32,
the first test is run. By convention, tests begin with the word TEST and
are descriptive and grammatical. The test method itself is in lines 35–43.
Finally, the SUMMARIZE method is called that prints out the number of tests
run, the number that succeeded, and the number that failed.

The test is simple: set sample 0 to a known value, call the compression
routine, and verify that the compressed data in packBuf is correct. The
returned value from COMPRESS is the number of bytes in packBuf or -1 if there
is an error; if there is no error, packBuf and comprCodeBuf are modified.

Listing 5-2 shows the code that does the actual work.

Listing 5-2. steim_spin0.spin: First Iteration of the Compression Code

```
 1  CON
 2        CODE08 = %01
 3        CODE16 = %10
 4        CODE24 = %11
 5  VAR
 6        long _nsmax
 7
 8  PUB INIT(nsmax)
 9  " Set the max length of the input samples array
10        _nsmax := nsmax
11
```

```
12   PUB COMPRESS(psampsBuf, ns, ppackBuf, pcomprCodesBuf) : ncompr
13   " Inputs :
14   "    psampsBuf - address of sampsBuf array (long array).
15   "    ns - length of 'sampsBuf' (number of samps to compress).
16   "    ppackBuf - address of 'packBuf' array (byte array) where
17   "                   samples are to be packed.
18   " pcomprCodesBuf - address of array of compresion codes
19   "                       (long array) - 16 codes per long.
20   " Output :
21   "    ncompr - length of packed array (bytes)
22        if ns == 0 'this isn't an error - but do nothing
23            return 0
24
25        if (ns < 0) | (ns > _nsmax)
26            return -1
27
28        ' handle sample0 first - it is always packed to
29        ' 3 bytes regardless of its size
30        bytemove(ppackBuf, psampsBuf, 3)
31        ncompr := 3
32        long[pcomprCodesBuf] := CODE24
33
34        if ns == 1
35            return ncompr
36        return -1
```

- **Lines 1–4:** Constants that define the compression codes.

- **Lines 8–10:** The initialization routine. Save a local version of NSAMPS_MAX.

- **Lines 12–21:** The compression method, along with comments detailing what the inputs and outputs are.

- **Lines 22–26:** Check the inputs.

- **Lines 30–32:** Perform the compression for the first sample.

- **Lines 34–35:** Return in the case of $N \equiv 1$.

- **Line 36:** Otherwise, return an error.

The actual compression is simple. We copy the three low bytes of sampsBuf[0] to packBuf[0]-packBuf[2], we set the compression code to reflect that this is a 3-byte packing, and we return the number 3. The calling code for COMPRESS is as follows:

```
nc := STEIM.COMPRESS(@sampsBuf, nsamps, @packBuf,
@comprCodeBuf)
```

The method definition is as follows:

```
PUB COMPRESS(psampsBuf, ns, ppackBuf, pcomprCodesBuf) : ncompr
```

MAIN passes in the *addresses* of the arrays; in particular, it passes the memory location of the first element of each array (@sampsBuf). The method definition saves those addresses as psampsBuf, and so on.

5.4 Passing Arrays to Methods

The compression method in the STEIM object must access the arrays sampsBuf, packBuf, and comprCodeBuf. To do so, it needs the address in hub memory where each of them is stored. The calling method is written thusly:

```
nc := STEIM.COMPRESS(@sampsBuf, nsamps, @packBuf,
@comprCodeBuf)
```

The symbol @sampsBuf is shorthand for "address of the first byte of the first sample of the sampsBuf array."

The definition of the called method in the STEIM object is as follows:

```
PUB COMPRESS(psampsBuf, ns, ppackBuf, pcomprCodesBuf) : ncompr
```

Here the variable psampsBuf holds that address. To access that data, we must inform the compiler that the variable is an address (rather than a value). In other words, to access the i-th sample (sampsBuf[i]), we must say long[psampsBuf][i]. Similarly, ppackBuf holds the address of the byte array packBuf, and it must be accessed as byte[ppackBuf][i]. To copy data from sampsBuf to packBuf, we must do something like the following:

```
bytemove(ppackBuf, psampsBuf, 3)
```

Here, 3 bytes are copied from the address psampsBuf (which is the address of the start of that array) to the address ppackBuf (which is the address of the start of the packBuf array).

The bytemove command copies 3 bytes from memory location psampsBuf to memory location ppackBuf (a longmove command would have moved 3 longs).

The expression long[pcomprCodeBuf] := CODE24 says to treat the address pcomprCodeBuf as a long and to write to all 4 bytes following that address.

A function/method definition in Spin looks like this:

```
1   VAR
2     long globalVar
3
4   PUB MYFUN(arg1, arg2) : retVal | localVar
5     ' globalVar is available for use and can be modified
6     ' globalVar changes will be seen outside the function
7     '
8     ' use arg1 and arg2 inside the function
9     '
10    ' localVar is available here and is local to the
11    ' function. It isn't available outside the function.
12    '
13    ' set the return value retVal
14  return ' this will return retVal to the calling program
```

The arguments arg1 and arg2, the return value retVal, and the local variable localVar are all optional.

5.5 Testing

Here are the tests that I run. As I was developing the code, I started out with the simpler tests (testing that sample 0 was packed correctly and then sample 1) and moved to successively more complex tests (sample 15, and so on).

```
TEST_THAT_SAMP0_IS_PROPERLY_PACKED
TEST_THAT_SAMP0_SETS_NCOMPR_CORRECTLY
TEST_THAT_SAMP0_SETS_COMPRCODE_CORRECTLY
TEST_THAT_COMPRESSOR_FAILS_FOR_NSAMPS_WRONG
```

```
TEST_THAT_SAMP1_IS_PROPERLY_PACKED_ONE_BYTE
TEST_THAT_SAMP1_IS_PROPERLY_PACKED_TWO_BYTES
TEST_THAT_SAMP1_IS_PROPERLY_PACKED_THREE_BYTES
TEST_THAT_SAMP1_SETS_COMPRCODE_CORRECTLY
TEST_THAT_SAMP1_SETS_COMPRCODE_CORRECTLY_TWO_BYTES
TEST_THAT_SAMP15_PACKS_PROPERLY
TEST_THAT_SAMP16_PACKS_PROPERLY
TEST_THAT_SAMP127_PACKS_PROPERLY

TEST_THAT_SAMP0_IS_PROPERLY_UNPACKED
TEST_THAT_SAMP1_IS_PROPERLY_UNPACKED
TEST_THAT_128_SAMPS_PROPERLY_COMPRESS_AND_DECOMPRESS
```

I built up the code by writing the test and then writing the code that lets the test succeed. As I built up the code bit by bit, I made sure *all* the tests were run every time I modified the program and that they all passed.

```
$ propeller-load -t -r -p /dev/cu.usbserial-A103FFE0 steim_
spin_Demo.binary
Propeller Version 1 on /dev/cu.usbserial-A103FFE0
Loading steim_spin_Demo.binary to hub memory
7568 bytes sent
Verifying RAM ... OK
[Entering terminal mode. Type ESC or Control-C to exit.]
Compression
mainCogId:     0

Test that sample 0 is properly packed to packBuf
...ok

<<<...output deleted...>>>

Test that compression and decompression of 128 random numbers
is successful
...ok
```

```
Tests Run: 20
Tests Passed: 20
Tests Failed: 0
```

5.6 Final Code

I won't go through the compression and decompression routines in detail because the focus of this book is on PASM (and they are quite self-explanatory). However, I reproduce them here because I'll refer to them when I am developing the PASM code.

5.6.1 Compression in Spin

The full compression code first checks that the inputs are correct. Next, the first sample is compressed, and then the remaining samples are differenced and compressed. The driver file (steim_spin1_Demo.spin) will call the code in Listings 5-3 and 5-4 (which are in file steim_spin1.spin).

Listing 5-3. steim spin1.spin: Complete Compressor Code Listing

```
1  PUB COMPRESS(psampsBuf, ns, ppackBuf, pcomprCodesBuf) : ↵
   ncompr | j, diff, adiff, codeIdx, codeShift
2  " Inputs :
3  "    psampsBuf - address of sampsBuf array (long array).
4  "    ns - length of `sampsBuf ` (number of samps to compress).
5  "    ppackBuf - address of `packBuf ` array (byte array) where
6  "                      samples are to be packed.
7  " pcomprCodesBuf - address of array of compresion codes
8  "                      (long array) - 16 codes per long.
9  " Output :
```

```
10    "    ncompr - length of packed array (bytes)
11         if ns == 0 ' this isn't an error - but do nothing
12             return 0
13
14         if (ns < 0) | (ns > _nsmax)
15             return -1
16
17         ' handle sample0 first - it is always packed to 3 bytes
18         ' regardless of its size
19         bytemove(ppackBuf, psampsBuf, 3)
20         ncompr := 3
21         long[pcomprCodesBuf] := CODE24
22
23         if ns == 1
24             return ncompr
25
26         repeat j from 1 to ns -1
27             diff := long[psampsBuf][j] - long[psampsBuf][j -1]
28             adiff := || diff
29             codeIdx := j / 16
30             codeShift := (j // 16) * 2
31             if adiff < $7F
32                 bytemove(ppackBuf + ncompr, @diff, 1)
33                 ncompr++
34                 long[pcomprCodesBuf][codeIdx] |= CODE08 << ↵
                     codeShift
35             elseif adiff < $7FFF
36                 bytemove(ppackBuf + ncompr, @diff, 2)
37                 ncompr += 2
```

```
38                        long[pcomprCodesBuf][codeIdx] |= CODE16 << ↵
                          codeShift
39              else
40                   bytemove(ppackBuf + ncompr, @diff, 3)
41                   ncompr += 3
42                   long[pcomprCodesBuf][codeIdx] |= CODE24 << ↵
                     codeShift
43
44        return ncompr
```

- **Lines 11–21:** Verify inputs and compress sample 0.

- **Line 27:** Form the backward difference $\delta_j = s_j - s_{j-1}$.

- **Line 28:** Calculate the absolute value $a_j = |\delta_j|$.

- **Lines 29–30:** The compression codes are 2 bits each, so the codes for samples s_j, $j = 0\text{–}15$ are in comprCodesBuf[0], the codes for samples s_j, $j=16\text{–}31$ are in comprCodesBuf[1], and so on. The j-th code is shifted by $(j \bmod 16) \times 2$ bits.

- **Lines 31-42:** Depending on whether a_j fits in 1, 2, or 3 bytes, place the difference in packBuf and place the code in comprCodeBuf.

5.6.2 Decompression in Spin

The decompression is a little more involved, mainly because negative numbers have to be sign-extended properly. The general outline is the same as for compression: handle the first sample and then loop through the remaining samples.

Listing 5-4. steim_spin.spin: Spin Decompression Method

```
1   PUB DECOMPRESS(psampsBuf, ns, ppackBuf, ncompr, ↵
    pcomprCodesBuf) : ndecomp | diff, pkIdx, codeIdx, ↵
    codeShift, theComprLong, jcomprCode, pkBytes, shneg
2   " Inputs :
3   "   psampsBuf - address of sampsBuf array
4   "   ns - length of 'sampsBuf' (number of samps to decompress)
5   "   ppackBuf - address of 'packBuf' array where samples ↵
    are packed
6   "   ncompr - length of packBuf
7   "   pcomprCodesBuf - array of compresion codes (16 codes ↵
    per long)
8   " Output :
9   "   ndecomp - number of samples decompressed (should be ↵
    same as ns)
10
11      ' check inputs
12      if ns == 0 ' this isn't an error - but do nothing
13          return 0
14
15      if (ns < 0) | (ns > _nsmax)
16          return -1
17
18      ' init
19      ndecomp := 0
20      pkIdx := 0
21
22      repeat while ns > ndecomp
23          ' codeIdx - index into the comprCodesBuf array
24          ' codeShift - index into the actual code long where
```

```
25              '   the code for this sample is stored
26              codeIdx := ndecomp / 16
27              codeShift := ( ndecomp // 16) * 2
28
29              theComprLong := long[pcomprCodesBuf][codeIdx]
30              jcomprCode := (theComprLong >> codeShift) & %11
31              case jcomprCode
32                  CODE08 :
33                      bytemove(@diff, ppackBuf + pkIdx, 1)
34                      diff <<= 24 ' sign extend
35                      diff ~>= 24
36                      pkBytes := 1
37                  CODE16 :
38                      bytemove(@diff, ppackBuf + pkIdx, 2)
39                      diff <<= 16 ' sign extend
40                      diff ~>= 16
41                      pkBytes := 2
42                  CODE24 :
43                      bytemove(@diff, ppackBuf + pkIdx, 3)
44                      diff <<= 8 ' sign extend
45                      diff ~>= 8
46                      pkBytes := 3
47
48          pkIdx += pkBytes
49          ncompr -= pkBytes
50
51          if ndecomp == 0 ' samp 0 is packed as is - not a ⏎
            difference
52              theSamp := diff
53          else
54              theSamp := long[psampsBuf][ndecomp -1] + diff
55
```

```
56            theSamp <<= 8
57            theSamp ~>= 8
58            long[psampsBuf][ndecomp] := theSamp
59            ndecomp++
60
61            if ncompr < 0 ' error check on ncompr
62                 return -1
63        return ndecomp
```

- **Lines 26–30:** Determine the compression code for this sample by getting the correct long from the comprCodesBuf array and then getting the appropriate 2 bits.

- **Lines 31–46:** Copy the difference bytes (either 1, 2, or 3, depending on the compression code for this sample) from packBuf and *sign-extend* them to form a proper 32-bit δ_j. The operations diff <<= 24 and diff ~>= 24 will first shift the low byte up to the high byte location and then do an *arithmetic* shift back to the low byte. An arithmetic shift retains the sign of the byte. So, if the low byte was a negative 1-byte number (-127 to -1), then the 32-bit number would still be negative (with 1s in all the high bits).

- **Lines 51–58:** Form the sample $s_j = s_{j-1} + \delta_j$ and sign-extend.

As we build up the PASM code, we have to reproduce each of these steps, including the loops.

5.7 The Need for Speed

The main reason to implement the code in PASM is to speed it up. Let's see how much time the compression and decompression take in Spin. Listing 5-5 shows the timing code in the driver file `steim_spin1_Demo.spin`.

Listing 5-5. Measuring the Timing of Compression

```
 1  PUB MAIN | t0, dt, j
 2  ...
 3    ' time
 4    nsamps := 128
 5    repeat j from 0 to nsamps-1
 6      sampsBuf[j] := j * 50000
 7
 8    t0 := cnt
 9    nc := STEIM.COMPRESS(@sampsBuf, nsamps, @packBuf, ↵
        @comprCodeBuf)
10    dt := cnt - t0
11    UARTS.STR(DEBUG, string(" nc= "))
12    UARTS.DEC(DEBUG, nc)
13    UARTS.PUTC(DEBUG, CR)
14    UARTS.STR(DEBUG, string(" dt= "))
15    UARTS.DEC(DEBUG, dt)
16    UARTS.PUTC(DEBUG, CR)
17    UARTS.STR(DEBUG, string(" dt(ms) ~ "))
18    UARTS.DEC(DEBUG, dt / ONE_MS)
19    UARTS.PUTC(DEBUG, CR)
20  ...
```

Running this code prints out the following:

```
...
nc= 382
dt= 1526096
dt (ms) ~ 19
```

Here, nc is the number of bytes in the compressed buffer packBuf, and the two dt values are the time taken to perform the compression (in clock cycles and milliseconds, respectively).

If your application is OK with taking 20ms to compress 128 samples, then you can stop right here. If not, let's estimate how much of a speedup we can expect in PASM.

5.7.1 Timing in PASM

Each instruction in PASM takes a fixed number of clock cycles that are documented in the manual. Almost all the instructions take four clock cycles exactly.[1]

A clock cycle is 12.5ns (when the system clock is running at 80MHz), so typically instructions require 50ns to complete.

The system clock is determined by the constants shown in Listing 5-6 in the main Spin file.

Listing 5-6. Clock Mode Settings

```
1  CON ' Clock mode settings
2    _CLKMODE = XTAL1 + PLL16X
3    _XINFREQ = 5_000_000
```

---

[1]There are exceptions. Hub operations (rdlong, for example) take between 8 and 23 clock cycles. There are a small number of other exceptions. The manual lists the timing for each instruction.

_XINFREQ is the frequency of the external crystal. The _CLKMODE variable sets the clock to 16 times the crystal frequency (in this case, 80MHz).

5.7.2 PASM Timing Estimate

During the compression, there is some setup, and then all the samples are processed.

For each of the 128 samples, something like the following must happen:

- Read a sample from the hub (~20 clock cycles).

- Subtract from the previous one (~5 instructions, ~20 cycles).

- Take the absolute value (~5 instructions, ~20 cycles).

- Check for the length of the absolute value (~10 instructions, ~40 cycles).

- Calculate the compression code location (~5 instructions, ~20 cycles).

- Write up to 3 bytes to the hub (~60 cycles).

The initialization and finalization may look something like this:

- Initialize the variables (~10 instructions, ~40 cycles).

- Take care of the overhead, in other words, writing the compression code to the hub every 16 samples, or 8 times for 128 samples (~20 cycles × 8 ~ 160 cycles).

The total is approximately 25,000 clock cycles, or 0.3ms (with an 80MHz clock). This is a speedup factor of 60, so if the data rates in your application are high, it will be worth going to the trouble of implementing it in PASM (in Figure 5-2, I show an example of things that go at different speeds!).

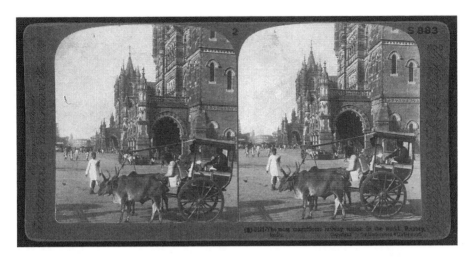

Figure 5-2. *Bullock cart in front of Victoria Terminus ("The most magnificent railway station in the world," Bombay, India, 1903.* `https://upload.wikimedia.org/wikipedia/commons/f/f4/` `Victoriaterminus1903.JPG.`

5.8 Summary

In this chapter, we worked through a full example of using Test-Driven Development to build and verify a Steim compressor and decompressor. The code is pure Spin, with a driver file (with a Demo suffix) and a worker file with functions (also known as *methods*) that are called from the driver. The tests are in the driver file, and each one exercises one small part of the specification.

I showed how a function/method is defined and called, how to test the inputs for reasonableness, how to copy bytes out of a long, and how to correctly copy them back in during decompression. I discussed how to pass variables and arrays to a Spin function and how to get a return value.

Finally, you learned how measure the time taken to process an array.

PART II

Spin and PASM

CHAPTER 6

Propeller Assembler: PASM

Now that we are all up to speed on Spin, let's plunge into PASM. Here I introduce the form and structure of PASM cogs and the details of PASM instructions.

In addition, I spend some time talking about how to pass information from the main cog (generally the driver program in Spin) to the PASM cogs. In this chapter and the next one, we will need to pass all the same variables (nsamps, sampsBuf, etc.) to the PASM cog as we did in the Spin version.

Remember, the cogs are almost completely independent of each other. To communicate between two of them, they have to agree on a location in hub memory where the shared information is kept. In addition, each cog has to continually check that location in case the other one has changed it.

Passing parameters between Spin programs is easy.

```
...
PUB MAIN
    retval := MYFUN(x, y, @z)

PUB MYFUN(funx, funy, funzPtr) : funret

    ...
    funret := ...
    return funret
```

© Sridhar Anandakrishnan 2018
S. Anandakrishnan, *Propeller Programming*, https://doi.org/10.1007/978-1-4842-3354-2_6

We simply place a list of the variables in the call (MYFUN(x, y, @z)), and those variables are available in the function body. Similarly, the function can return a number (funret), which is available in the main program.

It is more complicated in PASM because the PASM code is running in a separate cog that has its own memory. Spin code affects hub memory, and Spin instructions have *implicit* access that space. PASM code running in a separate cog has to *explicitly* access hub memory. That dance is what we will focus on for the rest of the book.

There is one more subtle difference between Spin and PASM: Spin functions (MYFUN) spring into existence *when they are called*, and they proceed from the beginning to the end and then disappear. A PASM cog is generally started once, and then it persists forever. You have to explicitly ask it to do something and have it idle otherwise.

Once launched, a PASM cog runs independently. The only way to pass parameters back and forth to the cog is to change a variable in hub memory and to have the cog read and react to that change.

6.1 Instructions in PASM

Cog memory consists of a series of longs (up to 496 of them). Some of those longs are instructions, and some are space reserved for variables. Instructions are executed in order starting at the first one (the one marked with ORG 0). You can request that instead of executing the next instruction, the Propeller should jump to a different part of cog memory. The Propeller will do so and then continue to execute instructions starting there.

There are more than 100 instructions in PASM, but many of them are close cousins, so don't be intimidated by the PASM manual. For example, there are five variants of add, four versions of sum, and so on. What all the instructions have in common is that they do one simple thing to a memory location in cog memory (sometimes referred to as a *register*). They *may* also affect the special flags Z and C. That's it.

The form of a PASM instruction is as follows:

```
<label> <if-clause> instr destination, <#>source <effect>
```

Here, the items in angle braces are optional. instr is the PASM instruction; the destination and source numbers are 9-bit values that refer to a register address. If the source is preceded by the optional *literal operator* #, then the source is that 9-bit value (rather than a register address). The label, if clause, and effect parts of the instruction are all optional.

Listing 6-1 shows a complete PASM program to toggle a pin (this is from p. 239 of the Propeller manual, v1.2).

Listing 6-1. Toggle a Pin in PASM

```
1   {{ AssemblyToggle.spin }}
2   CON
3      _clkmode = xtal1 + pll16x
4      _xinfreq = 5_000_000
5
6   PUB Main
7   { Launch cog to toggle P16 endlessly }
8       cognew (@Toggle, 0)          'Launch new cog
9
10  DAT
11  {Toggle P16}
12            org   0                'Begin at Cog RAM addr 0
13  Toggle  mov   dira, Pin         'Set Pin to output
```

```
14                      mov    Time, cnt        'Calculate delay time
15                      add    Time, #9         'Set minimum delay here
16   :loop              Waitcnt Time, Delay     'Wait
17                      xor    outa, Pin        'Toggle Pin
18                      jmp    #:loop           'Loop endlessly
19
20   Pin    long   |< 16                        'Pin number
21   Delay long    6_000_000                    'Clock cycles to delay
22   Time          res 1                        'System Counter space
23   FIT 496
```

- **Lines 1–8:** The Spin program in cog 0 that launches a new cog to do the work.

- **Line 8:** The Spin command to start a new cog using the code at the address @Toggle.

- **Lines 10–23:** The PASM code that does the work of toggling the pin.

- **Line 13:** This line has a *label* (Toggle), an *instruction* (mov), a *destination* register, and a *source* register (dira and Pin, respectively).

- **Line 15:** This line has a *literal value* (#9).

- **Line 16:** This line has a label and a *process control* instruction, waitcnt, that pauses the cog until the counter value in cnt reaches the value in the register Time. When the counter reaches the value in the register Time, the processor continues to the next expression. In addition, `waitcnt Time, Delay` will add `Delay` to `Time` and store that number in `Time`, so the next time the `waitcnt` instruction is executed, the processor will pause until time `Time + Delay`.

- **Line 18:** Another process control statement that changes the direction of execution. The instruction loops back to the instruction labeled `:loop` rather than stepping to the next instruction.

- **Lines 20–21:** Register holding data. The construct `|< 16` sets pin 16 of the register `Pin`.

- **Line 22:** Register of reserved workspace. Its value is undefined.

The new cog is loaded with nine longs. The first six longs are instructions (`mov`, `mov`, `add`, `waitcnt`, `xor`, and `jmp`); the next three longs are the data and reserved space. Execution begins with the first instruction and steps along sequentially, until it encounters the `jmp`. This is a basic program but one that captures many features of PASM. We will look at *effects* and hub interactions soon.

6.1.1 The Add Instruction

One of the most common tasks for a computer is to do arithmetic. In Spin you can write the following:

```
x += y
z++
a := b + c
```

You can do the same in PASM. Here is the add instruction:

```
' PASM version of x += y
add _cX, _cY
```

This sums the two numbers in variables _cX and _cY and places the result back into _cX.

```
' PASM version of z++
add _cZ, #1
```

Here the instruction increments the number in _cZ by 1 and places the result back into _cZ:

```
' PASM version of a := b + c
mov _cA, _cB
add _cA, _cC
```

Here we encounter the big difference between Spin and PASM. In Spin, we simply said a := b + c. Under the hood, two things are going on: b and c are added, and then the result is placed into a. In PASM, there is no "hood." We have to do those two things explicitly!

The mov _cA, _cB instruction moves the contents of variable _cB into _cA. Then the add instruction adds _cC to _cA and places the result back into _cA (and because we had the foresight to place _cB into _cA first, the result is as we desire).

6.1.2 The mov Instruction

The mov instruction sets a variable to a value.

```
' PASM version of x := y
mov _cX, _cY
```

Here we copy the contents of variable _cY to the variable _cX.

```
' PASM  version of x := 42
mov _cX, #42
```

Here we set _cX equal to 42. When you want to set _cX to a number, you have to tell PASM that by including the *literal* indicator (#). Without that, the instruction is mov _cX, 42 (don't do this at home!), and the Propeller would try to move the contents of *memory location 42* into _cX—not what you wanted.

```
' PASM version of x := 31415
'mov _cX, #31415 ' NOPE NOPE NOPE won't work
mov _cX, _cPiFour
```

Unfortunately, if you want to refer to numbers larger than 511 (in other words, any number that won't fit into 9 bits), you have to first store that number into a variable and then copy the contents of that variable to where you want it.

6.1.3 Variables

Variables are longs that are stored in cog memory along with the instructions (after all the instructions). You can initialize these variables to any number (any number that will fit in a long, of course).

```
_cPiFour long 31415
r0 res 1
r1 res 1
_cArr res 8
FIT 496
```

Here we declare a name for the variable (_cPiFour), followed by the size of the variable (long), followed by the value to which that variable is initialized (31415). Here you don't need the literal indication (#), and you aren't limited to 9 bits.

Finally, the line r0 res 1 reserves one long and places that address in r0. The form of this instruction is like this: the name of the variable (r0) followed by the res directive, followed by the number of longs to reserve.

The expression _cArr res 8 reserves eight longs and places the address of the first long in the variable _cArr. Any variables you refer to in your PASM code *must* have an associated storage declaration (either a line like _cPiFour long 31415 or a reservation line like r0 res 1). The PASM compiler will complain if you don't do this.[1]

The expression FIT 496 should always come at the end of the PASM program. It validates that the previous instructions and memory allocations fit within the allowed 496 longs.

6.1.4 Effects

Most instructions can include *effects*. If you specify either wz or wc, the Z or C flags will be changed, respectively. So, for example, the mov instruction has the following effects (this is an excerpt from the manual page for mov):

mov *Destination*, <#>*Value*

...

> If the WZ effect is specified, the Z flag is set (1) if
> *Value* equals zero. If the WC effect is specified, the
> C flag is set to *Value*s MSB. The result is written to
> *Destination* unless the NR effect is specified.

Here are some examples:

```
mov r0, #0 wz ' set Z=1
mov r0, #1 wz ' set Z=0
neg r0, #1    ' put -1 into r0
mov r1, r0 wc ' set C=1 (msb of r0 is 1)
mov r0, #42 wz,nr ' set Z=0 (wz), but don't change r0 (nr)
```

---

[1]res lines *must* come after long variable declaration lines.

The value of Z or C will persist until it is next changed by a wz or wc effect in an instruction. An important use of the effect is in branching and conditional expressions where an instruction is executed based on the value of these flags.

6.1.5 Literals

The mov instruction moves a value into a destination register. The source value either can be from another register or can be a literal value.

```
mov Destination, <#>Value
```

Literals are indicated by the pound sign (#) and are limited to 9 bits.

```
mov r0, r1 ' move contents of register r1 to register r0
mov r0, #0 ' set r0=0
mov r0, #42 ' set r0=42
'mov r0, #31415 ' ILLEGAL. Literals must be less than 512
```

6.1.6 Labels

There are 496 longs of cog memory available for use. Every instruction occupies one long. An instruction can include a *label* so that you can branch to that instruction.

```
...
  mov r1, #0
  mov r0, #8
:loop
  add r1, #1
  djnz r0, #:loop

_cPiFour long 31415
r0 res 1
r1 res 1
FIT 496
```

Here the label `:loop` labels the `add` instruction so that the jump instruction (`djnz r0, #:loop`) will execute the add instruction eight times (`djnz r0, #:loop` means "decrement the register `r0` and jump to label `:loop` if the result is nonzero").[2]

6.1.7 Conditional Evaluation

In Spin the following is a common task:

```
' conditional evaluation
' if x is less than 100, set x to y.
if x < 100
  x := y
x++
```

As you can imagine, there is quite a bit under the hood here that will need to be done explicitly in PASM. The general scheme is this: compare a variable with a number and either jump past a section of code or don't jump past it based on the result of the comparison.

```
1    cmp _cX, #100 wc
2    if_nc jmp #:done
3        'PASM instructions to evaluate if x < 100
4    mov _cX, _cY
5  :done
6    add _cX, #1
```

---

[2]There are two types of labels: global and local. Local labels have a colon as the first character. There are rules about the use of local variables that allow you to reuse the name, but I prefer to always use unique local variable names. See p. 242 in the Propeller manual if you want to reuse local variable names.

- **Line 1:** Compare x to 100 and set the C flag if $x < 100$.

Here is the explanation for cmp from the manual:

> CMP (Compare Unsigned) compares the unsigned
> values of Value1 and Value2. The Z and C flags, if
> written, indicate the relative equal, and greater or
> lesser relationship between the two. If the WZ effect
> is specified, the Z flag is set (1) if Value1 equals
> Value2. If the WC effect is specified, the C flag is set
> (1) if Value1 is less than Value2.

We ask for the wc effect, so if x (Value1) is less than 100 (Value2), then
the C flag will be set (C=1).

- **Line 2:** This is conditional expression that says that if
  the C flag is *not* set (if_nc), then execute the instruction
  that follows on that line (the jmp #:done). In our case, if
  $x < 100$, then the C flag will be set, and the jump will *not*
  be executed.

There are a host of if_xx conditional expressions. They all have similar
form (see p. 244 of the Propeller manual for a complete list).

- if_z instr: If the Z flag is set, execute the instruction.

- if_nz instr: If the Z flag is *not* set, execute the
  instruction.

- if_c instr: This is the same as the previous one, but
  for the C flag.

- if_nz_and_nc instr: If the Z flag is *not* set and the C
  flag is also *not* set, then execute the instruction...and
  every possible combination of Z, NZ, C, NC, AND, and OR.
  As you can imagine, this gives tremendous flexibility in
  deciding when to do something.

I used the cmp instruction to set the C flag. Remember, every instruction gives you the option to manipulate the Z and C flags, so you can set the groundwork for the various if_ instructions in many ways.

6.1.8 Branching

As I said earlier, the Propeller will execute instructions in order starting at the start of cog memory. It will proceed to the next instruction unless the order is interrupted by a *jump* instruction. There are two jump instructions that we will use a lot.

- jmp #:label: Jump to an address labeled :label immediately.

- djnz r0, #:label: Decrement the variable r0 and jump to a label if the result is not zero.

These are used in conditional evaluation (as in the previous section) and in loops. In Spin, you would say this:

```
x := 0
repeat 8
  x++
```

In PASM, you must set up a loop variable (here r0) and explicitly decrement and check its value. Repeat until its value is zero.

```
1    mov r0, #8
2    mov _cX, #0
3    :loop
4      add _cX, #1
5      djnz r0, #:loop
```

In line 5, the instruction is to "decrement r0 and jump to :loop if the result is not zero." After eight iterations, r0 will be zero, and the loop is exited.

6.2 Reading the PASM Manual

PASM *instructions* are composed of (up to) four parts. For example, the instruction to move the contents of a 4-byte long from hub memory to cog memory is rdlong (the manual page for rdlong is shown in Figure 6-1).

rdlong _cns, _cnsPtr wz

The parts of the instruction are as follows:

- The action to be taken (rdlong).

- The destination address (_cns).

- The source address.

- The effect wz, which will affect the Z flag. There is also wc, which affects the C flag.

- The effect nr, which will prevent the instruction from actually occurring but only set the Z or C flag.

In the manual page, the important pieces of information are the succinct description of the instruction:

Instruction   Read long of main memory.

Here's the summary:

RDLONG *Value*, <#> *Address*

- *Value* (d-field) is the register to store the long value into.

- *Address* (s-field) is a register or a 9-bit literal whose value is the main memory address to read from.

Here is the detailed explanation, along with a description of the wz, wc, and nr *effects*:

RDLONG syncs to the hub. ...If the WZ effect is specified, the Z flag will be set (1) if the value read from main memory is zero.

Finally, the time taken to execute the instruction will be stated. For most instructions, it is four clock cycles. Hub instructions take longer because of the need to sync with the other cogs.

RDLONG is a hub instruction. Hub instructions require 8 to 23 clock cycles to execute....

6.3 Categories of PASM Instruction and Registers

There are a large number of PASM instructions and registers, but they fall into a small number of categories, which I summarize here.

6.3.1 Copying

The instructions in this category are used to both copy values from one memory location to another, as well as to affect the Z and C flags. The instruction mov d, <#>s <wz> <wc> will move the source (either the contents of register s or the value #s) into register d. If the source value is zero and the wz effect is specified, then set the Z flag. If the wc effect is specified, then the C flag is set to the source's MSB (either 0 or 1).

RDLONG – Assembly Language Reference

RDLONG

Instruction: Read long of main memory.

RDLONG *Value*, ⟨#⟩ *Address*

Result: Long is stored in *Value*.

- *Value* (d-field) is the register to store the long value into.
- *Address* (s-field) is a register or a 9-bit literal whose value is the main memory address to read from.

Opcode Table:

–INSTR– ZCRI –CON– –DEST– –SRC–	Z Result	C Result	Result	Clocks
000010 001i 1111 ddddddddd ssssssss	Result = 0	—	Written	8..23

Concise Truth Table:

In					Out		
Destination	Source	Z	C	Effects	Destination [1]	Z [2]	C
s–––– ––––; –	s–––– ––––; –	–	–	wz wc	long value	0	0

[1] Destination Out is always generated since including an NR effect would turn RDLONG into a WRLONG instruction.
[2] The Z flag is cleared (0) unless Destination Out equals 0.

Explanation

RDLONG syncs to the Hub, reads the long of main memory at *Address*, and stores it into the *Value* register. *Address* can point to any byte within the desired long; the address' lower two bits will be cleared to zero resulting in an address pointing to a long boundary.

If the WZ effect is specified, the Z flag will be set (1) if the value read from main memory is zero. The NR effect can not be used with RDLONG as that would change it to a WRLONG instruction.

RDLONG is a hub instruction. Hub instructions require 8 to 23 clock cycles to execute depending on the relation between the cog's hub access window and the instruction's moment of execution. See Hub on page 24 for more information.

Figure 6-1. *Manual page for rdlong*

6.3.2 Arithmetic

There are a number of math instructions to take the absolute value, add or subtract two numbers, or negate a number. There are variants of each of these that do slightly different things based on the value of flags.

- The add instruction adds the *unsigned* values in the destination and source and places the result in the destination register. By contrast, adds treats the values as signed numbers. The instructions addx and addsx are *extended* additions that let you do multilong addition (for example, 64-bit addition; see the manual for details).

- There are a similar set of subtraction instructions (sub, subs, subabs, etc.)

- The neg instruction negates a number; negc does so if C=1; negnc does so if C=0; and negz and negnz negate based on the value of the Z flag.

6.3.3 Boolean, Comparison, and Bit-Shift Operators

These instructions operate bitwise.

- The Boolean instructions and, or, and xor perform the bitwise *and, or,* and *exclusive or* of the destination and the source, placing the result in the destination register. test performs an *and* but doesn't store the result in the destination; this is usually done to affect the flags.

- The comparison operator cmp d, s compares the destination and the source (treating them as unsigned values). If the wz effect is specified, then Z=1 if d=s. If the wc effect is specified, then C=1 if d<s. There are other comparison instructions (cmps, cmpsub, cmpsx, etc.) that compare signed values or compare and subtract, and so on.

- The min and max operators store the greater or lesser of the source and destination in the destination register, respectively.

There are a number of bit-setting and shifting operators.

- The mux... family of operators sets the destination register based on two things: the high bits in the source and the value of either C or Z. Thus, muxc d, #5 will set bits 2 and 0 (because #5 = b0101) of the destination register d to the value of the flag C. The other bits in d are unaffected. The other members of this family are muxnc, muxz, and muxnz.

The bit shifting operators are as follows:

- **Reverse:** rev d, s reverses the lower $32 - s$ bits of d and stores the result in d. So, if $s = 24$, then reverse the lower 8 bits of d and clear the upper 24 bits. Store this result back into d.

- **Rotate:** rol d, s rotates the destination register (d) left by s bits, placing the MSBs rotated out of d into its LSBs. Similarly, ror will rotate right. By contrast, rcl d, s also rotates the register d left but fills the LSBs with the value of C. rcr does the same for rightward rotation.

- **Shift:** shl d, s shifts d left by s bits. The new LSBs are set to zero. Similarly, shr shifts right.

- **Shift arithmetic:** sar d, s shifts d right by s bits, extending the MSB. In other words, the value of MSB will be copied into all the shifted bit locations. Thus, sar d, #8 will set the upper 8 bits to either 1 or 0 depending on the original value of the MSB of d. The lower 24 bits of d are the result of the shift.

6.3.4 Process Control

Process control instructions will either pause the processor until a condition is met or alter the sequence of execution.

The waitcnt t, dt instruction will pause execution until the internal counter cnt is equal to the value in t. When the two are equal, the value of t will be set to t+dt, and the processor will step to the next instruction. Because cnt is a 32-bit register that rolls over, the pause from the waitcnt instruction will eventually end, but it could take up to 4 billion counts (about 53 seconds at 80MHz clock) if t happens to be less than the current value of cnt.

The reason that the time register t is incremented by dt is to allow for regular and deterministic delays in the program. With this mechanism, regardless of when you call waitcnt, the program will step every dt seconds.

The instruction waitpeq value, mask will pause execution until the values in the ina register referenced by the high bits in mask are equal to the bits in value. In other words, if, for example, mask=b0100 and value=b0100, then the processor will pause until pin 2 is high.[3] Similarly, waitpne will wait until the mask bits in input register ina are *not equal* to those bits value.

The jmp and djnz instructions alter the direction of execution. Normally, the next instruction is executed. At a jmp #:location, the next instruction to be executed will be the one labeled :location. The instruction djnz d, #:loop will decrement the number in d and will jump to :loop if d≠0. Otherwise, the instruction next in line will be executed. tjz and tjnz are similar, but they only test the value of d without decrementing it.

---

[3]This is how we generally use waitpeq, though we could have multiple pins in mask, and we could have both highs and lows in the values for those pins.

6.3.5 Hub Reads/Writes

The hub has more (but slower) memory than the cogs. You can read and write longs, words, or bytes from and to the hub.

The read instruction rdlong cogmem, hubmem will read a long from hub memory address hubmem and store that value in the cog location cogmem. The wrlong cogmem, hubmem instruction will write a long from cogmem to hubmem. Similarly, rdword, rdbyte, wrword, and wrbyte operate on words and bytes.

6.3.6 Locks

Locks (or *semaphores*) are a special utility to allow cogs to negotiate exclusive access to some resource. There are eight lock IDs (0–7) in the Propeller that can be checked out and released. After creating a lock with locknew lockID, which stores a lock ID number in lockID, you can request a lock with lockset and release the lock with lockclr.

The way locks work is that a cog has to first create a lock and get its ID. This ID has to be shared with the other cogs. Next, both cogs will request a lock. One (and only one) of the cogs will get it. (The one that asks for it first; because locking is a hub operation, the cogs ask for the lock one after the other in round-robin fashion, so there is no possibility of conflict.) The cog that gets the lock can then, for example, access a shared memory location. The other cogs don't have the lock, so they will simply loop continuously requesting the lock until the cog with the lock releases it.

If a lock is set, then its value is 1; if it is available, then its value is 0.

lockset lockID wc sets the value of lockID to 1 and returns the *previous* value of the lock (in the C flag).

If nobody else had checked out the lock, then its value will be 0; the lockset will set the lock to 1 and set C=0 (because that is its previous value). If somebody else has the lock, then its value will be 1; lockset will set C=1.

A cog calls lockset and then checks the value of C. If C is 0, then that cog has the lock; if it is 1, then it doesn't have the lock.

If a cog does have the lock, it must make sure to eventually call lockclr lockID.

6.3.7 Variables

In addition to the instructions (each of which takes up one long), you can declare and initialize variables or reserve blocks of space. Always put the res directives at the end of the code.

```
_cVarname long 31415 ' these declare and initialize the vars
_cVarAns  long 42    ' variables are always longs in PASM

_cArry    res 8      ' this reserves 8 longs
```

6.3.8 Special Registers

Each cog has 16 special registers, each of which is a long (4 bytes). Because a cog has 512 longs of memory, this leaves 496 longs for instructions and variables.

- cnt: The 32-bit system counter is incremented by 1 at every system clock. This register will roll over when it fills up ($2^{32} - 1$ counts, or approximately 4 billion). With an 80MHz clock, that happens every 53 seconds. This is a read-only register.

- dira: This register sets the direction for the signals on the pins. The 32 bits of this register correspond to the 32 pins (P0 to P31). If a bit is a 1, then the corresponding pin is an output. *All cogs have their own dira register.* Thus, a pin is an output if *any* cog declares it so; it is an input if *no cog* declares it as an output.

- outa: If a pin is set as an output in the dira register, then this register can control its value. Setting a bit high (1) in outa will set the corresponding pin high. Any cog that has declared a pin as an output can control it. So, it is up to the programmer to avoid conflicts.

- ina: The value of each bit in this register reflects the state of the physical pin. If pin PN is high, then bit N of ina will be high. Again, this pin will be an input only if no cog has set it as an output.

- par: This register is populated by the cognew command when the cog is launched. The second argument to cognew is (generally) an address in hub memory, and that address is placed in par so that the cog can communicate with other cogs.

6.3.9 Counters

I don't discuss the registers ctra, phsa, and frqa in this book, but together they provide a powerful and general-purpose counting capability. You can do a remarkable number of things with these registers, including pulse width measurements, counting the number of pulses, pulse-width modulation (PWM), frequency synthesis and measurement, and much more. See the app note at https://www.parallax.com/downloads/an001-propeller-p8x23a-counters for details.

6.4 The Structure of PASM Programs

These programs run from two files: a "driver" file called, for example, myprog_Demo.spin (Listing 6-2 shows the outline for such a file) and a worker file called myprog.spin (Listing 6-3). The driver file is pure Spin code, but the worker file is a combination of Spin and PASM code. The driver file will have overall control of the program, such as for opening the terminal and starting and stopping cogs. The worker file (or files) will be responsible for a single cog and will generally have a few Spin methods along with the PASM code. At a minimum, it will have the following:

- **INIT:** Set up the needed variables.

- **START:** Start a new cog and load the PASM code into it.

- **STOP:** Stop the cog.

In addition, the worker file will have a section of PASM code that will be loaded into a new cog by the START method.

Listing 6-2 shows the driver file myprog_Demo.spin.

Listing 6-2. Structure of Spin Driver File

```
 1  {*
 2   * myprog_Demo.spin : do an important thing
 3   *}
 4
 5  CON ' Clock mode settings
 6  ...
 7  CON ' Pin map
 8  ...
 9  CON ' UART ports
10  ...
11  OBJ
12    MYPROG : "myprog" ' load the worker file
13  VAR
14  ...
15
16  PUB MAIN
17  ...
```

```
18  ' initialize and start the worker
19  MYPROG.INIT
20  MYPROG.START
21  ...
22  ' stop the worker
23  MYPROG.STOP
```

- **Line 12:** Read the file myprog.spin and make it
  available as MYPROG.

- **Line 19–23:** Call functions INIT, START, and STOP in the
  library MYPROG.

Listing 6-3 shows the worker file myprog.spin.

Listing 6-3. Structure of PASM Worker File

```
1  {*
2   * myprog.spin : spin and pasm worker code
3   *}
4  CON
5  ...
6  VAR
7  ' set up some local variables. At a minimum, keep track of ⏎
   the cog id
8  byte myprogcogid, mylocalvar
9
10 ' initialize vars, at a minimum set the cog id to -1 ⏎
   (indicating that no
11 ' cog is running this code)
12 PUB INIT
13    mylocalvar := 0
14    myprogcogid := -1
15
```

```
16  ' start a new cog (after stopping the old one)
17  ' save the cog id as well as returning it
18  PUB START
19    STOP
20    myprogcogid := cognew(@MYPROG, @mylocalvar)
21    return myprogcogid
22
23  ' stop the cog - after checking that it is running.
24  ' else do nothing
25  PUB STOP
26    if myprogcogid <> -1
27      cogstop(myprogcogid)
28
29  ' actual PASM code (loaded into new cog by the cognew ↵
    command in START)
30  DAT ' myprog
31  MYPROG ORG 0
32    ' get the address of the variable to be passed here
33    mov _cmyvarPtr, par
34    ' get the value of that variable
35    rdlong _cmyvar, _cmyvarPtr
36    ...
37
38
39  ' reserve space for the address and value of the variables
40  _cmyvarPtr res 1
41  _cmyvar res 1
42
43  FIT 496
```

- **Line 8:** These variables are available inside this file to all the functions.

- **Lines 12, 18, 25:** A public function can be called from outside this file (for example, from the driver file, myprog_Demo.spin). A public function is written as PUB INIT, and a private function (one that can be called only from within this file) is written as PRI APRIVATEFUNCTION.

- **Lines 12–14:** The INIT function that initializes variables.

- **Lines 18–121:** The START function first stops the new cog (if it is running) and then starts it. The cognew command takes two arguments: the address of the PASM code and the address of a local variable, which is passed to the PASM cog. The function returns the number of the newly launched cog.

- **Lines 30–43:** The PASM code that is copied to a new cog and run.

- **Line 30–31:** The special operator DAT announces the start of the PASM code. The line MYPROG ORG 0 assigns a name (MYPROG) to that code and says that it starts at address 0 in the cog. (This is always the case in this book, though it doesn't have to be; code could start anywhere within the 496 longs of the cog, but that is advanced voodoo!)

- **Lines 33–41:** These lines are the way parameters get passed to the code. You'll learn more about that in the next sections.

- **Line 43:** This line always ends the PASM code.

101

6.5 Passing Parameters to PASM

A significant challenge in PASM programming is exchanging data between cogs and between Spin and PASM cogs. There are two main ways this is done.

- An address in hub memory is passed to a cog when it is launched. The instruction cognew(@PROG, @var) will place the address of var into the special register PAR when the PASM cog PROG is run.

- An address in hub memory is placed into cog memory before the cog is launched.

This is discussed at length in Sections 8.3 and 8.4.

6.6 Summary

PASM instructions have four parts: the instruction itself (mov, add,...), the destination, the source, and an optional *effect* (wc or wz) that sets the value of the C and Z flags.

To communicate between cogs, both cogs must have the address of a variable that they regularly check. That address is passed to a new cog on launch in the PAR register.

```
1  VAR
2    'variable1 and variable2 are stored in successive locations
3    long variable1, variable2
4
5  PUB MAIN
6    ' cognew command will store the address of variable1
7    ' in PAR and then launch MYCOG in a new cog
8    cognew(@MYCOG, @variable1)
9
```

```
10   DAT
11   MYCOG org 0
12      mov _cvar1Ptr, par ' when mycog is launched, ↵
                           ' par contains the ↵
13                         ' address of variable1
14      mov _cvar2Ptr, par ' the next long location contains the ↵
                             address
15      add _cvar2Ptr, #4 ' of variable2
16
17      rdlong _cvar1, _cvar1Ptr ' the actual value of variable1
18      ' is obtained by a rdlong
19      rdlong _cvar2, _cvar2Ptr
```

CHAPTER 7

Interacting with the World

One of the main uses of a Propeller is to "talk" to hardware such as motors, relays, switches, LEDs, and so on. In the Propeller there are 32 general-purpose input/output pins, P0–P31. Figure 7-1 shows an overview of the relationship between the cogs and pins. Pins P30 and P31 are usually reserved for the programming and serial ports. Pins P28 and P29 are usually tied to an electrically erasable programmable read-only memory (EEPROM) that stores the program even when there is no power applied. So, pins P0–P27 are available for general input/output use.

Again, I must emphasize that all the cogs can run in parallel, so they can interact with the pins at the same time. If a cog has declared a pin an input, then it can read the value of that pin *at the same time as other cogs do*. If a pin is declared an output by more than one cog, then the output of that pin is the logical OR of the output of those cogs.

Three registers control these pins.

- DIRA is a 32-bit register that controls the direction of the pin associated with each bit. If bit N of this register is 1, then the corresponding pin P<N> will be an output, and if it is zero, that pin will be an input.

© Sridhar Anandakrishnan 2018
S. Anandakrishnan, *Propeller Programming*, https://doi.org/10.1007/978-1-4842-3354-2_7

- OUTA is a 32-bit register that sets the value of a pin P<N> by setting or clearing the associated bit N. These pins will be affected only if the value of the associated DIRA bit is set to output (1).

- INA is a 32-bit register that reflects the value of the signal on pin P<N>. A low voltage (0–0.7V) is a zero on the associated bit N of the register, and a high voltage (2.7–3.3V) is a 1. Again, bitN of DIRA should be set to input (0).

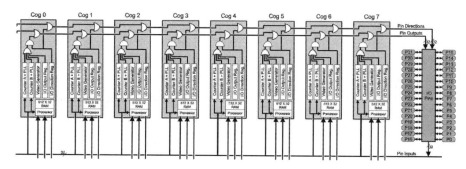

Figure 7-1. *Block diagram of the Propeller showing the cogs and pins*

All eight cogs have access to all of the pins. Each of the cogs has its own independent DIRA, INA, and OUTA registers. The output of a pin is what is "agreed on" by all the cogs. If more than one cog declares a pin as output, then the pin will be high if *any of those* cogs sets it high. The pin will be low if *all of those* cogs set it low. In Figure 7-2, a switchman is manually operating a switch that controls which track a train will take.

Figure 7-2. *Switchman throwing a switch at the Chicago and NW Railroad Proviso yard, Chicago, IL, 1942. Photo by Jack Delano; available at the Library of Congress Farm Security Administration archives.* `www.loc.gov/pictures/item/fsa1992000705/PP/`.

A pin will be an input if *no active cog has it as an output.*

To view the result of setting a pin, a logic analyzer is useful. A logic analyzer attaches to a pin and displays the *logical* state of the pin as a function of time (1 or 0). Unlike an oscilloscope, you can monitor multiple pins (usually 8 or 16), and importantly, the logic analyzer software is aware of common protocols such as Universal Serial Receive/Transmit (UART), Serial Peripheral Interface (SPI), Inter-Integrated Communication (I2C), and so on. (I am partial to the Logic8 from Saleae.[1]) See also the Papilio Logic Analyzer.[2]

---

[1]`https://www.saleae.com`
[2]`http://store.gadgetfactory.net/papilio-fpga-logic-analyzer-kit/`

7.1 Outline

In this chapter we will read and set the value of pins in both Spin and PASM. We will look at the SPI communication protocol (a common method for communicating between embedded devices). We will implement SPI between cogs as a way to log data from a PASM cog to the main Spin code. Finally, I introduce the concept of *semaphores* or *locks* that allow two cogs to interact without confusion or conflict. This is a dense chapter, so feel free to refer to it if and when you need it!

7.2 Timing in Spin and PASM

Instructions in Spin run slowly compared to the same instruction in PASM (by an order of magnitude or more). In addition, in Spin, the amount of time an instruction takes to complete is subject to change. By contrast, the timing of PASM instructions is short (generally four clock cycles) and unvarying. For applications that require precise and rapid timing (high-frequency clocks or monitoring a high data rate line), PASM is preferred. Each PASM instruction has a known number of clock cycles to complete.

```
1  CON ' Clock mode settings
2    _CLKMODE = XTAL1 + PLL16X
3    _XINFREQ = 5_000_000
4
5    ' system freq as a constant
6    FULL_SPEED = ((_clkmode - xtal1) >> 6) * _xinfreq
7    ' ticks in 1ms
8    ONE_MS = FULL_SPEED / 1_000
9    ' ticks in 1us
10   ONE_US = FULL_SPEED / 1_000_000
```

- **Lines 2–3**: These define the clock speed of the Propeller. _XINFREQ is the frequency of the crystal oscillator. _CLKMODE is a register that sets the CLK register to (in this case) generate a clock that is 16 times the oscillator frequency.

- **Line 6**: Here we define a constant for the number of clock ticks in one second. It is somewhat cryptic, but in short, XTAL1 and PLL16X are predefined constants. The expression _CLKMODE - XTAL1 = PLL16X = 0x40_00.

Therefore, PLL16X >> 6 = 16 (right shift by 6 bits). Finally, multiply that by the oscillator frequency. This is a reliable way to get the *startup* clock speed.

7.3 Spin

In Spin these registers are usually set as shown in Listing 7-1.

Listing 7-1. Toggle a Pin in Spin (ch7/io0.spin)

```
1   CON
2     BLUE = 10 ' blue led
3
4   PUB MAIN
5     DIRA~ ' set all pins low (no output)
6     OUTA[BLUE] := 0 ' set pin 10 low
7     DIRA[BLUE] := 1 ' set pin 10 to output
8     repeat
9       ! OUTA[BLUE] ' toggle pin 10
10      PAUSE_MS(1000)
```

- **Line 5**: The tilde (~) *after* a variable says to set that variable to zero.

- **Line 7**: When the array form of addressing (arr[j]) is used with a register (DIRA[BLUE]), the effect is to address individual bits. In this case, only bit 10 of DIRA is set to 1, so P10 is set to output.

- **Line 9**: The exclamation mark (!) is a bitwise negation of the bit OUTA[BLUE], which will toggle pin P10.

- If we wish to read the value on a line, the Spin code is shown in Listing 7-2:

Listing 7-2. Read a Switch and Pin (ch7/io1.spin)

```
1  CON
2    SW = 11 ' normally open, high
3    SWMASK = |< SW ' set pin <SW> high
4    INPIN = 12
5
6  PUB MAIN | val
7    DIRA~ ' set all pins low (no output)
8
9    ' initially wait until switch is open (high)
10   waitpeq(SWMASK, SWMASK, 0) ' wait until high
11   repeat
12     waitpne(SWMASK, SWMASK, 0) ' wait for it to go low
13     val := INA[INPIN]
14     waitpeq(SWMASK, SWMASK, 0) ' wait for release of switch
```

- **Line 3**: Set bit 11 of SWMASK high. The operator |< is referred to as a "Decode" operator that sets the bit corresponding to the number in SW.

- **Line 10**: SWMASK is used in two ways here: waitpeq(*Value*, *Mask*, 0). The first argument to waitpeq (*Value*) is the value that the Propeller will compare against the values of the input pins that are set in the *Mask* argument. In other words, bit 11 is 1 in *Value*; bit 11 is 1 in *Mask*. Compare the value 1 to bit 11 of INA, and wait until they are equal, that is, until P11 is high.

- **Line 12**: Similar to waitpeq, waitpne waits until the *Value* argument is *not equal* to the pins set in *Mask*. Bit 11 of *Value* is 1, so wait until P11 is *not* 1.

- **Line 13**: To read the value of a line, simply read the value of a bit of the INA register.

7.4 PASM

In PASM the same registers (DIRA, OUTA, and INA) are available at the addresses (unsurprisingly) dira, outa, and ina. These addresses are registers in the reserved part of the cog. Recall that when a cog is launched, 512 longs are copied to the cog RAM, of which the last 16 longs are reserved registers (including our old friend par).

7.4.1 Toggle a Pin in PASM

Similar to the Spin code in Listing 7-1, we toggle the value of a pin once a second but using PASM, as shown in Listing 7-3.

Listing 7-3. Toggle a Pin in PASM (ch7/io2-pasm.spin)

```
1   ...
2   ' << ADD THESE LINES
3   CON
```

```
 4    BLUE = 10
 5    SW = 11
 6    INPIN = 12
 7    ONESEC = ((_clkmode - xtal1) >> 6) * _xinfreq
 8
 9  VAR
10    ...
11    byte rdpinCogId ' << ADD THIS
12
13  PUB MAIN
14    ...
15    ' << ADD THESE LINES
16    rdpinCogId := cognew (@RDPIN, 0)
17    UARTS.STR(DEBUG, string (" rdpinCogId : "))
18    UARTS.DEC(DEBUG, rdpinCogId)
19    UARTS.PUTC(DEBUG, CR)
20    UARTS.PUTC(DEBUG, LF)
21
22  ' << ADD THESE LINES
23  DAT ' RDPIN
24
25  RDPIN ORG 0
26    mov dira, #0 wz ' set all pins to input
27    muxnz outa, _cblueMask ' set pin low
28    muxz dira, _cblueMask ' set led pin to output
29
30    mov r0, cnt
31    add r0, _coneSec
32  :loop
33    waitcnt r0, _coneSec
34    xor outa, _cblueMask
```

```
35    jmp #:loop
36
37  _cblueMask long |< BLUE
38  _cswMask long |<SW
39  _coneSec long ONESEC
40  r0 res 1
41  FIT 496
42
43  ' Program ends here
```

- **Line 26**: Set all pins to input. The wz effect will set Z.

- **Line 27–28**: Set pin BLUE (10) low before setting it to be an output. The muxnz outa, _cblueMask instruction says to set the pins in outa that are referenced in _cblueMask to the value of NOT Z (outa[_cblueMask] := !Z. In other words, pin 10 is set in _cblueMask, so set pin 10 of outa to !Z, which is 0. muxz sets dira[_cblueMask] := Z, which sets pin 10 to be an output.

- **Lines 30–33**: Set r0 to the current counter value plus one second worth of counts. Wait until the counter reaches that value (waitcnt will increment r0 by _coneSec when it expires so it is ready for the next waitcnt).

- **Line 34**: Toggle the output pin 10. xor outa, _cblueMask is the bitwise exclusive OR of the value of the output pins and the mask register (which has pin 10 set high). The result is written back to outa. So, if outa[10] == 1, then 1 XOR 1 = 0, and outa[10] is set to zero. If outa[10] == 0, then 0 XOR 1 = 1, and outa[[10] is set to one.

7.4.2 Monitor a Switch

As in Listing 7-2, we monitor a switch and then read the value of a pin when the switch closes, as shown in Listing 7-4.

Listing 7-4. Read a Pin in PASM (ch7/io2-pasm.spin)

```
1   CON
2     BLUE = 10
3     SW = 11
4     INPIN = 12
5     ONESEC = ((_clkmode - xtal1) >> 6) * _xinfreq
6
7   DAT
8   STEIM ORG 0
9
10    mov dira, #0 wz ' set all pins to input
11    waitpeq _cswMask, _cswMask
12  :loop
13    waitpne _cswMask, _cswMask
14    test _cinMask, ina wc
15    rcl _cval, #1
16    waitpeq _cswMask, _cswMask
17    jmp #:loop
18
19  _cblueMask long |< BLUE
20  _cswMask long |<SW
21  _cinMask long |< INPIN
22  _coneSec long ONESEC
23  r0 res 1
```

- **Line 11**: As in the Spin code, `waitpeq Value, Mask` waits until the pins in `INA` that are referenced in `Mask` are equal to `Value`."

- **Line 13**: `waitpne` waits until `Mask` is *not equal* to the value.

- **Lines 14–15**: To read a pin, `test _cinMask, ina wc` will set C flag to the bitwise AND of the mask and the ina register. `rcl _cval, #1` will move the C flag into the low bit of `_cval`.

7.5 Communication Protocols

There are number of common ways to send data from one device to another on a small number of lines, including UART, I2C, and the 1-Wire protocols. These are commonly classed as *serial* communication channels because the bits are transmitted over time. In contrast, a *parallel* channel would use a number of lines to send the bits at the same time. In Figure 7-3, an early serial communication device is shown: an electric telegraph which would visually display the signal transmitted from the other end.

Figure 7-3. *Five-needle electric telegraph invented by Charles Wheatstone (of the Wheatstone bridge), 1837. The telegraph was used to signal when trains arrived and left stations. Now at the London Science Museum. Photo by Wikipedia user* Geni; *license CC-BY-SA GFDL.*

A widely used serial protocol for interdevice communications is the SPI bus. The SPI protocol requires four lines for bidirectional communications between a so-called master and multiple slave devices. The SPI protocol uses a bitwise data transmission mechanism, with a bit sent by both sides (and that bit received by the other side) at each SPI clock cycle. The SPI clock frequency is typically a few hundred kilohertz to a few megahertz. Here we will use an 8kHz clock.

SPI communications are bidirectional, but one of the two ends is designated the *master,* and the other is the *slave.* The master will control the timing of the transfer by generating the select signal and the SPI clock, and the slave will read from the master.

The slave will also write to the master at the same time. Therefore, the master cannot set a pace that is too fast for the slave to keep up with.

SPI is fundamentally quite simple (though the devil is in the details). To send a number from master to slave, the master indicates the beginning of the transfer by pulling the select line low. It then toggles a clock and makes sure that each successive bit of the number is ready on the active edge of the clock (generally the rising edge). After the bits are all sent, the master pulls the select line high. At the other end, the slave waits until the select line is low. It then watches the clock line and receives a bit at each active edge. The end of the transfer is signaled by the select line going high.

- **Select**: The select or chip select (CS) line (active low) selects the slave devices with which the master wants to communicate and determines the start and end of communications. The master device generates this signal.

- **Clock**: The SPI clock line (SCLK) controls the timing of data transmission. The most common arrangement is for the rising edge of the clock to be the one at which data is exchanged and the falling edge is when the two sides are free to change the data on that line. The master device generates the clock.

117

- **Data out**: The data out or master out or master out/ slave in (MOSI) line is where the data from the master to the slave is placed. The master device will ensure that a data bit is stable on the line prior to the rising edge of the clock. This is because on the rising edge, the slave device reads the value. The master should keep the data on this line stable until the falling edge because the slave could read it at any time between the rising and falling edges.

- **Data in**: The data in or master in or master in/slave out (MISO) line is where data from the slave to the master is placed. The master will read the MISO line on the rising edge of SCLK. Thus, at each rising edge of SCLK, a bit is sent from master to slave and from slave to master.

The interpretation of the bits (whether big- or little-endian, number of bits, and so on) is entirely up to agreement between the slave and the master. Figure 7-4 shows the case where we have 8 bits. The red lines are the *active edges* at which the MOSI line is read by the slave. The blue lines are when the master can change the value of the MOSI line in preparation for the next active edge.

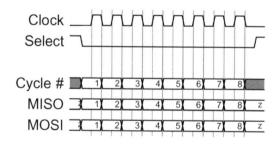

Figure 7-4. *SPI timing diagram for the case when the clock starts out low (CPOL=0) and the data is required to be valid on a rising edge (CPHA=0)*

7.6 SPI Logging

The values on the pins can be set by any cog and read by any cog. That means we can use them to communicate *between cogs*. We will use that as a logging facility where the PASM cog will write to the SPI bus and the Spin cog will read from it. As the Spin cog is slower, it must control the transactions. In other words, the PASM cog is the master, and the Spin cog is the slave.

We are going to write an SPI logging utility. The Spin cog (main) will request a log value, and a PASM cog (logtst) will transmit the log value. The main cog will read that value and print it out. The handshaking between the cogs is as follows:

- The PASM cog will block, waiting for the REQ line to be asserted (set to the active level, in this case raised).

- When the main cog (the slave) is ready to receive a log value, it will raise the REQ line.

- This will signal the PASM cog (the master) to initiate an SPI transfer by lowering the CS line (the CS line is active low, so it is *asserted* by lowering it).

- The falling CS line will signal the main cog to lower the REQ line so that no further SPI transfers start until the main cog has finished with the current one and has successfully printed the value.

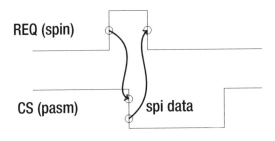

Figure 7-5 shows the output of a logic analyzer (LA). The LA can monitor and trigger on individual lines (here I triggered on REQ on channel 0). In addition, logic analyzers can interpret well-known communication protocols such as the RS-232 serial protocol, the I2C protocol, and, as in this case, the SPI protocol. I have informed the LA of the four SPI lines, the endianness and length of the data, and the phase and polarity of the clock; the LA can interpret the data on the MOSI and MISO lines and display the result. In this example, the MOSI line is showing a 32-bit number that was transmitted MSB first and is interpreted as 0x2A.

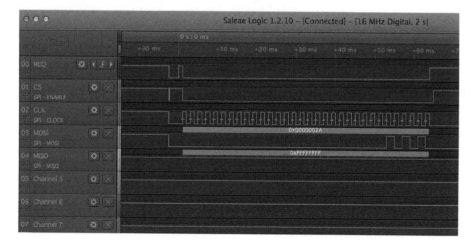

Figure 7-5. *Logic analyzer display*

In the Spin code (Listing 7-5), we define the pins, start the spitst cog, and assert the REQ line. When the CS line is asserted by the PASM cog, we read the log value and then re-assert the REQ line.

Listing 7-5. SPI Logging, Spin Side (ch7/spi-log Demo.spin)

```
1   ...
2   CON
3     REQ = 0
4     CS = 1
5     CLK = 2
```

```
 6    MOSI = 3
 7    MISO = 4
 8
 9    CSMASK = |<CS
10    CLKMASK = |<CLK
11  VAR
12    byte logCogId
13
14  ...
15
16  PUB MAIN | x, x0, logVal
17    ...
18    logCogId := -1
19
20    ' set the REQ line low, then set it as an output line
21    ' all others are inputs
22    outa[REQ] := 0
23    dira ~ ' all lines in
24    dira[REQ] := 1 ' req out
25
26    SPILOG.INIT
27    logCogId := SPILOG.START
28    UARTS.STR(DEBUG, string(CR, LF, " logCogId : "))
29    UARTS.DEC(DEBUG, logCogId)
30    UARTS.PUTC(DEBUG, CR)
31    UARTS.PUTC(DEBUG, LF)
32
33    ' wait here until PASM cog sets CS line high
34    waitpeq(CSMASK, CSMASK, 0)
35
36    ' OK ready for SPI
37    outa[REQ] := 1 ' assert req
```

```
38    repeat
39      ' wait for cs mask to go low
40      waitpne(CSMASK, CSMASK, 0)
41      !outa[REQ] ' lower req
42      logVal := READ_SPILOG 'read 32 bits
43      UARTS.HEX(DEBUG, logVal, 8) ' print out logVal
44      UARTS.PUTC(DEBUG, CR)
45      UARTS.PUTC(DEBUG, LF)
46      !outa[REQ] ' raise req and loop
```

- **Lines 3–7**: Define pins.

- **Lines 22–24**: Set all pins to input for main cog, except for REQ.

- **Lines 26–27**: Launch the SPILOG PASM cog.

- **Line 34**: Make sure CS is high (that is, not currently in an SPI transfer). Assert REQ.

- **Lines 40–46**: Wait until the CS line is lowered by the PASM cog, immediately de-assert the REQ line, read a log value, and print it. Raise the REQ line to signal that the main cog is ready for another log value. Repeat.

The actual SPI read is done with the method shown in Listing 7-6.

Listing 7-6. Method to Read 32 Bits from SPI

```
1  PUB READ_SPILOG : logVal | b
2    logVal := 0
3    repeat 32
4      waitpeq(CLKMASK, CLKMASK, 0)
5      b := INA[MOSI]
6      waitpne(CLKMASK, CLKMASK, 0)
7      logVal <<= 1
8      logVal |= b
```

The actual SPI read is straightforward; it waits for the clock line to go high (`waitpeq`), reads a bit (`b := INA[MOSI]`), and shifts it into `logVal`, as follows:

```
1  logVal <<= 1
2  logVal |= b
```

- **Line 1**: Shift the bits in `logVal` left by one position.

- **Line 2**: b is the value read earlier (either 0 or 1). By OR-ing it with `logVal`, we set the lowest bit to the value of b.

The `waitpne` instruction is there so that we wait until the clock line goes low before looping so that we don't read the same bit twice.

7.6.1 PASM SPI Write

The core of the PASM SPI write is shown in Listing 7-7 and the code following the listing, with two subroutines that set the pins and do the actual writing.

Listing 7-7. SPI Logging, PASM Side (ch7/spi-log.spin)

```
1  DAT 'spilog
2  SPILOG  ORG 0
3
4     call #SETUP_PINS
5
6     mov _clogVal, #42
7     call #WRITE_SPI
8     ...
```

- **Line 4**: Set up the REQ pin as input and the SPI pins as outputs.

- **Lines 6–7**: Place the log value to be transmitted into
  _clogVal and call WRITE_SPI to transmit. WRITE_SPI
  will wait for REQ to be raised and will then transmit
  _clogVal on the SPI lines.

The subroutine to set the pins (SETUP_PINS) is shown in Listing 7-8.

Listing 7-8. Subroutine to set the SPI pins' direction

```
1   SETUP_PINS
2     mov dira, #0, wz
3
4     muxz outa, _ccsMask 'preset cs high, and then to output
5     muxz dira, _ccsMask
6     muxnz outa, _cclkMask ' preset clk low
7     muxz dira, _cclkMask
8     muxnz outa, _cmosiMask ' preset mosi low
9     muxz dira, _cmosiMask
10  SETUP_PINS_ret ret
```

- **Line 2**: Set all pins to inputs.

- **Lines 4–5**: Set CS high and then set CS to output.

- **Lines 6–9**: Set CLK and MOSI low and then set them to
  output.

In Listing 7-9, we do the actual work of writing 32 bits to the MOSI line.
First we wait for the REQ line to be asserted, then we loop 32 times, setting
the MOSI line appropriately (with a short wait between bits).

Listing 7-9. Subroutine to transmit the data on MOSI

```
1   WRITE_SPI
2     waitpeq _creqMask, _creqMask
3     mov r0, #32 wz ' Z is set = 0
```

```
4    mov _cdt, cnt
5    add _cdt, _cEighthMS
6    waitcnt _cdt, _cEighthMS
7
8    ' lower cs
9    xor outa, _ccsMask
10
11   ' tx 32 bits, msb first
12   :spiloop
13     rol _clogVal, #1 wc ' set C from high bit of logVal
14     muxc outa, _cmosiMask ' set mosi to C
15
16     muxnz outa, _cclkMask ' raise clock (Z=0 from above)
17     waitcnt _cdt, _cEighthMS
18     xor outa, _cclkMask ' lower clock
19     waitcnt _cdt, _cEighthMS
20     djnz r0, #:spiloop
21
22     ' raise cs
23     xor outa, _ccsMask
24   WRITE_SPI_ret ret
25   ...
26   _cdt long 0
27   _cOneSec long ONE_SEC
28   _cOneMS long ONE_MS
29   _cOneUS long ONE_US
30   _cEighthMS long ONE_MS >> 3
31
32   _creqMask long |<REQ
33   _ccsMask long |<CS
34   _cclkMask long |<CLK
35   _cmosiMask long |< MOSI
```

- **Line 13**: Set the loop index and set Z to zero.

- **Lines 14–16**: Set_cdt to the current counter, add 1/8ms (125us), and wait until then. waitcnt takes two arguments, and the counter will wait until it is equal to the first argument. It will then add the second argument to the first so that you can call waitcnt again.

- **Line 19**: Lower CS. xor outa, _ccsMask will toggle the CS.

- **Line 23–24**: Get the bits, with the most significant bit first, and place it on the MOSI line. The rol _clogVal, #1 wc instruction will rotate left and put the highest bit in C. The instruction muxc outa, _cmosiMask will set MOSI to C.

- **Lines 26–29**: Raise the clock line, wait 1/8th of a millisecond, lower the clock, wait again, and loop.

- **Line 33**: Lower the CS.

7.6.2 Logging Deadlock

Warning!   If you call WRITE_SPI, you must have another cog that raises the REQ line; otherwise, you will block forever.

At any time you can call WRITE_SPI in the PASM code. It will block until the Spin code raises the REQ line. At that point, the PASM code will transmit the log value and continue.

7.7 Locks

On single-track lines, railroads needed a foolproof way to prevent two trains from traveling on the same section of track at the same time. They settled on a simple but elegant solution: the semaphore. A brass cylinder or token is cast and engraved with the name of the stations at each end of the section of single-track. A train could enter that section *if and only if* the engineer had physical possession of the token. When he arrived at the station at the far end, he would give the token to the station master, who could pass it on to a train traveling in the other direction.

You still see a version of this when road crews are working on potholes and signals at each end control the traffic.

7.7.1 Introduction to Locks

The propeller has semaphores for the same reason: to control access to *critical shared resources*. To prevent a collision (for example, one cog is modifying an array at the same time that another is reading from it), the propeller has eight semaphores. In Figure 7-6, we see a semaphore that controlled the movement of trains in order to prevent collisions.

- locknew/lockret: Create or destroy a semaphore.

- lockset: Request the semaphore. If it is free (semaphore = 0), set the state of the semaphore to 1 and return a 0 (obtaining the lock). If it isn't free (semaphore = 1), return a 1 (*not* obtaining the lock). You must check the return value to know whether you obtained the lock or not.

- lockclr: Set the state of the semaphore to 0, releasing the semaphore.

Figure 7-6. *Waiting for the signal, Santa Fe RR Train, Melrose, NM. Photo by Jack Delano, 1943. From the Library of Congress Farm Security Administration archives.* `http://www.loc.gov/pictures/item/fsa1992000785/PP/.`

Here is a sketch of the process, with time proceeding to the right. ("Time" is a bit of misnomer here; because locking is a hub operation, even though both cogs may request the lock at the same time, the hub will service those requests in order.) At time 1, cog 0 acquires the lock. Because lockset is a hub operation, only one cog a time can request the lock. Though it looks like both cogs are competing for the lock, in fact only of them can obtain it. In this case, cog 0 received the lock, and when cog 1 requested it (one clock cycle later), it was informed that somebody else had the lock (because lockset returns 1). Remember, the propeller operates in round-robin fashion for hub operations, providing exclusive access to the hub for one cog, then the next, and so on.

At time 2, cog 1 again requests the semaphore, and the Propeller again returns the *previous* state of the lock, 1, which indicates that somebody else has it. This continues until time 5, when cog 0 releases the semaphore, and it is set to 0. At time 6, cog 1 again requests the lock, and this time the *previous* value is 0, so cog 1 knows that it has the semaphore.[3] It holds it until time 9.

cog0	set				clr				
0	1	1	1	1	0	1	1	1	0
cog1	set	set	set	set	set	set			clr
0	1	2	3	4	5	6	7	8	9

The semaphore is created, and then a lockset/lockclr pair of instructions brackets the critical section of code. So, for example, in our code, cog 0 could acquire samples between times 1 and 5, but we must prevent cog 1 from attempting to compress them during that time. Between times 6 and 9 the compression can safely proceed.

---

[3] I lie. In reality, cog 0 would have released the cog at time 5, and during the next clock cycle, cog 1 would have requested and received the lock, but for illustration purposes, I fibbed.

The way we have written the code, there is in fact no chance of a collision between sample acquisition and compression. The main cog *blocks* while the compression cog is working, so it is impossible for it to modify sampsBuf. However, that isn't very good design. It is wasteful for main to sit there twiddling her thumbs while steim is off doing his job. She could be (and usually is) performing other tasks. It is under that type of system design that the semaphore is most useful. After all, if one has a multicore parallel machine, we might as well use it as a…multicore…parallel…machine!

7.7.2 Using Locks for Logging

We could, for example, use a semaphore to signal between cogs. If you don't want to waste an I/O line for the REQ signal between cogs for logging, you could use a semaphore instead, as shown here in Listing 7-10:

Listing 7-10. Demonstration of using locks for SPI signalling

```
1   PUB MAIN
2
3   ...
4     logSem := locknew
5     repeat until not lockset(logSem) 'acquire semaphore
6     COMPR.START ' start the pasm cog
7   ...
8
9     lockclr(logSem) ' release the semaphore, allowing PASM access
10    repeat
11      waitpne(CSMASK, CSMASK, 0)
12      logVal := READ_SPILOG
```

```
13    waitpeq(CSMASK, CSMASK, 0)
14    repeat until not lockset(logSem)    ' re - acquire ↵
      semaphore
15    UARTS.STR(DEBUG, string(" Log value : "))
16    UARTS.HEX(DEBUG, logVal, 8)
17    UARTS.PUTC(DEBUG, CR)                    ' release semaphore
18    lockclr(logSem)
```

- **Lines 4–9**: Create a new semaphore, acquire it, and start the PASM cog. When ready to start logging, release it.

- **Lines 11–13**: Read a log value on the SPI lines.

- **Line 14**: lockset will return TRUE if somebody else has the token. In that case, repeat until won't exit. Eventually, the other person will release the semaphore, lockset will return FALSE, repeat until will terminate, and control will continue.

- **Lines 15–18**: We now have the token and can slowly print out the log value, *confident that the PASM cog won't try to send another value.*

- **Line 18**: Release the semaphore so that the PASM cog can acquire it when it is ready to send another log value.

This is the code in the Spin section that interfaces with the locks (Listing 7-11).

Listing 7-11. Spin code that uses locks to signal SPI communications

```
1    ' in the pasm cog, we must somehow pass the semaphore ↵
     number (logSem)
2    ' to the cog: _clogSem
3    ...
```

131

```
 4
 5  WRITE_SPI
 6  :semLoop                       ' acquire semaphore
 7    lockset _clogSem wc
 8    if_c jmp #:semLoop
 9
10    ' <<WRITE LOG VALUE TO SPI >>
11    lockclr _clogSem       ' release semaphore
```

- **Lines 6–8**: In the PASM cog, the WRITE_SPI function will check whether the semaphore is free. If so, it will acquire it, *confident that the Spin cog is ready.*

  This loop will repeat as long as somebody else has the token. When nobody else has the token, C=0, and we continue to transmit the log value on the SPI lines.

- **Line 8**: Once we are done, release the semaphore.

7.8 Some Common Tasks

Here are some examples of common operations, with both Spin and PASM equivalents shown. As can be seen, some things are much simpler in Spin. This must be weighed against the speedup that can be achieved with PASM.

7.8.1 Assignment

Spin	PASM
x := 42	mov _cX, #42
y := 31415926	mov _cY, _cbigNum
	_cbigNum long 31415926

7.8.2 Multiplication

Spin	PASM	
z := x * y	1	shl _cX, #16
	2	mov r0, #16
	3	shr _cY, #1 wc
	4	:loop
	5	if_c add _cY, _cX wc
	6	rcr _cY, #1 wc
	7	djnz r0, #:loop

The multiply code is from Appendix B of the Propeller manual. Two 16-bit numbers, _cX[0..15] and _cY[0..15] are multiplied, and the result is saved to _cY.

Let $x = 42$ and $y = 2$. Here are their binary representations:

```
31 30 29 28 27 26 25 24 23 22 21 20 19 18 17 16 15 14 13 12 11 10  9  8  7  6  5  4  3  2  1  0
```

x:	0 0 0 0 0 0 0 0 0 0 0 0 0 0 0 0 0 0 0 0 0 0 0 0 0 0 1 0 1 0 1 0
y:	0 0 0 0 0 0 0 0 0 0 0 0 0 0 0 0 0 0 0 0 0 0 0 0 0 0 0 0 0 0 1 0 |C|

After shl _cX, #16, here is what they look like:

x':	0 0 0 0 0 0 0 0 0 0 1 0 1 0 1 0 0 0 0 0 0 0 0 0 0 0 0 0 0 0 0 0
y:	0 0 0 0 0 0 0 0 0 0 0 0 0 0 0 0 0 0 0 0 0 0 0 0 0 0 0 0 0 0 1 0 |C|

After shr _cY, #1 wc, here they are again:

x':	0 0 0 0 0 0 0 0 0 0 1 0 1 0 1 0 0 0 0 0 0 0 0 0 0 0 0 0 0 0 0 0
y:	0 0 0 0 0 0 0 0 0 0 0 0 0 0 0 0 0 0 0 0 0 0 0 0 0 0 0 0 0 0 0 1 |0|

Loop 1 of 16

Because C=0, the add is not performed.

After rcr _cY, #1 wc, here is what they look like:

x': | 0 0 0 0 0 0 0 0 0 0 1 0 1 0 1 0 | 0 0 0 0 0 0 0 0 0 0 0 0 0 0 0 0 |

y: | 0 0 0 0 0 0 0 0 0 0 0 0 0 0 0 0 | 0 0 0 0 0 0 0 0 0 0 0 0 0 0 0 0 | |1|

Loop 2 of 16

Because C=1, the add is performed. The add has a wc effect, which will set C if the add overflows. In this case, C=0.

Here they are after the add:

x': | 0 0 0 0 0 0 0 0 0 0 1 0 1 0 1 0 | 0 0 0 0 0 0 0 0 0 0 0 0 0 0 0 0 |

y: | 0 0 0 0 0 0 0 0 0 0 1 0 1 0 1 0 | 0 0 0 0 0 0 0 0 0 0 0 0 0 0 0 0 | |0|

Here is the y register after rcr (the x' register is unchanged):

y: | 0 0 0 0 0 0 0 0 0 0 0 1 0 1 0 1 | 0 0 0 0 0 0 0 0 0 0 0 0 0 0 0 0 | |0|

From here on, y is shifted right once each iteration of the loop. No more adds are performed as all the remaining bits of y (bits 0–13) are 0.

Loop 16 of 16

The final result is $y = 42 \times 2 = 84$.

x': | 0 0 0 0 0 0 0 0 0 0 1 0 1 0 1 0 | 0 0 0 0 0 0 0 0 0 0 0 0 0 0 0 0 |

y: | 0 0 0 0 0 0 0 0 0 0 0 0 0 0 0 0 | 0 0 0 0 0 0 0 0 1 0 1 0 1 0 0 | |0|

7.8.3 Division

Spin	PASM
q := x / y	1 ' Divide x [31..0] by y [15..0]
'quotient (32 bit)	2 ' (y [16] must be 0)
r := x // y	3 ' on exit, quotient is in x [15..0]
'remainder (32 bit)	4 ' and remainder is in x [31..16]
	5 ' get divisor into y [30..15]
	6 shl _cY, #15
	7 ' ready for 16 quotient bits
	8 mov r0, #16
	9 :loop
	10 ' y =< x? Subtract it,
	11 ' quotient bit in c
	12 cmpsub _cX, _cY wc
	13 ' rotate c into quotient,
	14 ' shift dividend
	15 rcl _cX, #1
	16 ' loop until done
	17 djnz r0, #:loop
	18 ' quotient in x [15..0],
	19 ' remainder in x [31..16]

This is also from the appendix. Get a pad of graph paper and confirm for yourself how it works.

7.8.4 Loops

Spin	PASM
1 x0 := 0	1 mov _cx0, #0
2 x := 1	2 mov _cx1, #1
3 repeat 8	3 mov _cf, _cx1
4 f := x + x0	4
5 x0 := x	5 mov r0, #8
6 x := f	6 :loop
	7 add _cf, _cx0
	8 mov _cx0, _cx1
	9 mov _cx1, _cf
	10
	11 mov _clogVal, _cf
	12 call # WRITE_SPI
	13 djnz r0, #:loop

The critical parts are mov r0, #8, which sets the loop counter and djnz r0, and #:loop, which decrements r0 and jumps to :loop if the result is nonzero. When r0=0, continue past the loop.

7.8.5 Conditionals

Spin	PASM
if x => 10	1 cmp _cX, #10 wz, wc
x := 0	2 if_nz_and_nc jmp #:cont
' else	3 mov _cX, #0
	4
	5 :cont
	6 'else

The compare sets the Z flag if $X \equiv 10$ and the C flag if $X < 10$. So, if neither is set, then X must be greater than 10. The if_nz_and_nc jmp #:cont instruction will jump to :cont in that case.

7.9 Summary

Setting and reading pins are central tasks to the function of the Propeller. In PASM code you set and read pins by writing to the outa register and reading from the ina register, respectively. In general, you define a *mask* that is specific to a pin and then operate on that mask and the ina/outa registers.

In this book I try and document my code with comments and descriptive variable and method names. In addition I use TDD when possible. In Figure 7-7, is a picture of all the lubrication points on a locomotive: documentation and maintenance!

```
1     mov dira, #0 wz ' set all pins to input, and set z=1
2     ' mux <flag > <dest >, <source >
3     ' the mux__ instructions set the bits of
4     ' the <destination register > that are called out in the
5     ' <source register > baseed on the value of <flag >
6     '
7     ' for example, here we set outa based _coutMask
8     ' and NOT Z (!Z)
9     muxnz outa, _coutMask
10    ' here we set dira based on _coutMask and Z
11    muxz dira, _coutMask
12
13    ...
14    ' here we toggle the bit in outa based on _coutMask
15    xor outa, _coutMask
16
17    ...
18    ' here we set C from ina, based on the value of _cinMask
19    test _cinMask, ina, wc
```

Figure 7-7. *Locomotive lubrication chart, Chicago and NW Railroad Laboratory, Chicago, IL. Photo by Jack Delano, 1942. From the Library of Congress Farm Security Administration archives.* `www.loc.gov/pictures/item/fsa1992000662/PP/`.

CHAPTER 8

Implementing the Compression Code in PASM

In this chapter and the next one, we will start to write some real PASM code to implement the compression. In this chapter, I will talk mainly about passing parameters to the PASM cog. In the next chapter, I will complete the compression and decompression code.

8.1 Passing Parameters to PASM

To reproduce the Spin code from `steim_spin` in PASM, we need to have a way to pass the addresses of `sampsBuf` and other arrays to the PASM cog. In Spin that was simple. `@sampsBuf` was the address, and it could be passed to the `COMPRESS` method, where the values could be accessed with `long[psampsBuf][j]`.

There are two main ways to pass information back and forth. Let's begin with the (in my opinion) simpler way, which is passing information in the `cognew` command.

© Sridhar Anandakrishnan 2018

S. Anandakrishnan, *Propeller Programming*, https://doi.org/10.1007/978-1-4842-3354-2_8

We'll set up these files:

```
ch8/
    ├── steim_pasm0_Demo.spin
    └── steim_pasm0.spin
```

8.2 Setting Up steim_pasm0

Create two new files: steim_pasm0_Demo.spin (Listing 8-1) and steim_
pasm0.spin (Listing 8-2). Most of what is shown here is similar to what is in
the pure-Spin version, but the compression will be done in PASM instead.
First, we set up the ..._Demo.spin file, which is the entry point.

Listing 8-1. steim_pasm0_Demo: Spin Side of the First Iteration of
the PASM Compression

```
 1  {* -*- Spin -*- *}
 2  {* steim_pasm0_Demo .spin *}
 3
 4  CON ' Clock mode settings
 5    _CLKMODE = XTAL1 + PLL16X
 6    _XINFREQ = 6 _250_000
 7
 8    ' system freq as a constant
 9    FULL_SPEED = (( _clkmode - xtal1) >> 6) * _xinfreq
10    ONE_MS = FULL_SPEED / 1_000 ' ticks in 1ms
11    ONE_US = FULL_SPEED / 1 _000_000 ' ticks in 1us
12
13  CON ' Pin map
14
15    DEBUG_TX_TO = 30
16    DEBUG_RX_FROM = 31
17
```

```
18   CON ' UART ports
19     DEBUG = 0
20     DEBUG_BAUD = 115200
21
22     UART_SIZE = 100
23     CR = 13
24     LF = 10
25     SPACE = 32
26     TAB = 9
27     COLON = 58
28     COMMA = 44
29
30   OBJ
31     '1 COG for 3 serial ports
32     UARTS : "FullDuplexSerial4portPlus_0v3"
33     NUM : "Numbers" 'Object for writing numbers to debug
34     COMPR : "steim_pasm0"
35
36   CON
37     NSAMPS_MAX = 128
38
39   VAR
40     long nsamps, ncompr
41     long sampsBuf[NSAMPS_MAX]
42     long comprCodeBuf[NSAMPS_MAX >> 4]
43
44     byte mainCogId, serialCogId, comprCogId
45     byte packBuf[NSAMPS_MAX << 2]
46
47   PUB MAIN
48
```

```
49       ' main cog
50       mainCogId := cogid
51
52       ' uart cog
53       LAUNCH_SERIAL_COG
54       PAUSE_MS(500)
55
56       UARTS.STR(DEBUG, string(CR, " Compression ", CR, LF))
57       UARTS.STR(DEBUG, string(" mainCogId : "))
58       UARTS.DEC(DEBUG, mainCogId)
59       UARTS.PUTC(DEBUG, CR)
60       UARTS.PUTC(DEBUG, LF)
61
62       ' compression cog
63       COMPR.INIT(NSAMPS_MAX)
64       comprCogId := COMPR.START
65
66       UARTS.STR(DEBUG, string(" comprCogId : "))
67       UARTS.DEC(DEBUG, comprCogId)
68       UARTS.PUTC(DEBUG, CR)
69       UARTS.PUTC(DEBUG, LF)
70
71       nsamps := 1
72       ncompr := COMPR.COMPRESS (@sampsBuf, nsamps, ↵
         @packBuf, @comprCodeBuf)
73
74       UARTS.STR(DEBUG, string(" ncompr : "))
75       UARTS.DEC(DEBUG, ncompr)
76       UARTS.PUTC(DEBUG, CR)
77       UARTS.PUTC(DEBUG, LF)
```

```
78      repeat
79        PAUSE_MS(1000)
80
81  PRI LAUNCH_SERIAL_COG
82  " method that sets up the serial ports
83    NUM.INIT
84    UARTS.INIT
85    UARTS.ADDPORT (DEBUG, DEBUG_RX_FROM, DEBUG_TX_TO, -1, ↵
          -1, 0, %000000, DEBUG_BAUD) 'Add DEBUG port
86    UARTS.START
87    serialCogId := UARTS.GETCOGID 'Start the, ports
88    PAUSE_MS(300)
89
90  PRI PAUSE_MS(mS)
91    waitcnt(clkfreq /1000 * mS + cnt)
92
93  ' Program ends here
```

- **Line 34**: Import the file steim_pasm0.spin as object COMPR.

- **Lines 63–64**: Initialize and start the compression cog. As you will see, the COMPR.START function (a Spin function) launches a new PASM cog.

- **Lines 71–72**: Call the Spin method COMPR.COMPRESS (a Spin function), which signals the PASM cog to compress the samples in sampsBuf.

We will start by implementing the simplest possible compression code in Spin and PASM code in steim_pasm0. It includes passing nsamps to the PASM cog and reading ncompr back. As I said earlier, the PASM code has to monitor the hub memory and react to a change. Here we use nsamps as the trigger. If the value is greater than zero, then perform a compression, and at the end of the compression, set ncompr to a nonzero value. That, in turn, will be the signal to the Spin code that the PASM cog has completed its work. In this first example, that work is simple: you don't have to do anything! The compressor will simply set ncompr to a nonzero value and return to monitoring nsamps.

The steim_pasm0.spin file starts out looking like Listing 8-2.

Listing 8-2. First Version of steim_pasm0.spin Showing the Spin Methods and the Beginning of the PASM Code

```
 1   CON
 2        CODE08 = %01
 3        CODE16 = %10
 4        CODE24 = %11
 5
 6   VAR
 7        byte ccogid
 8        long mymax
 9
10        long myns, myncompr
11
12   PUB INIT(nsmax)
13        mymax := nsmax
14        ccogid := -1
15
16   PUB START
17        STOP
18        ' myns <> 0 controls when the compression is started
19        myns := 0
20        ccogid := cognew (@STEIM, @myns)
21        return ccogid
22
```

```
23  PUB STOP
24      if ccogid <> -1
25          cogstop (ccogid)
26
27  PUB COMPRESS(psampsBuf, ns, ppackBuf, pcomprCodeBuf) : ncompr
28  " Inputs : psampsBuf - address of long array of samples ↵
    (max len, mymax)
29  "'          ns - number of samples to compress
30  "           ppackBuf - address of byte array of packed data
31  "           pcomprCodeBuf - address of long array of ↵
                compression, codes
32  " Output : ncompr - number of bytes in packBuf
33  "
34  " Modified : packBuf and comprCodeBuf are changed
35
36      myns := 0
37      myncompr := 0
38
39      ' this will start the compression
40      myns := ns
41
42      ' when ncompr is non -zero, the compression is complete
43      repeat until myncompr > 0
44      return myncompr
45
46  PUB DECOMPRESS(psampsBuf, ns, ppackBuf, ncompr, ↵
    pcomprCodesBuf) : ndecomp
47      return 0
48
49  DAT 'steim
```

```
50    "
51    "
52
53  STEIM org 0
54     ' copy the param addresses
55     mov _cnsPtr, par
56     mov _cncomprPtr, par
57
58     add _cncomprPtr, #4
59
60  : mainLoop
61     ' the signal for starting the compression is when ns <> 0
62     rdlong _cns, _cnsPtr wz
63     if_z jmp #:mainLoop
64
65     ' signal completion
66     mov _cncompr, #3
67     wrlong _cncompr, _cncomprPtr
68
69     ' wait for another compression request
70     jmp #:mainLoop
71
72  ' const
73  _ccode24 long CODE24
74  _ccode16 long CODE16
75  _ccode08 long CODE08
76
77  _cnsPtr res 1
78  _cncomprPtr res 1
79
80  _cns res 1
```

```
81   _cncompr res 1
82
83   r0 res 1
84
85       FIT 496
```

- **Line 10**: The variables myns and myncompr are declared one after the other, so they will be stored in hub memory one after the other. This property of storage is used in the PASM cog to find these variables. In other words, be careful about rearranging variable declaration order!

- **Lines 16–21**: We start the compression cog with cognew (after stopping any already running cog). The command cognew(@STEIM, @myns) says to copy the code in the DAT section (lines 49–85) into a new cog and to launch that cog. In addition, the address of the variable myns (a hub address) is also passed to the cog.

- **Lines 27–44**: Here the actual compression will take place. When myns is set to a nonzero number, the compression cog will notice that and will then begin the compression. When the cog has completed the compression, it will set myncompr, the length of the packed buffer packBuf, to a positive number.

- **Lines 46–47**: The decompression routine does nothing for now.

- **Lines 53–58**: This is the heart of the *parameter passing* to the cog. The address of myns (a hub address) is copied to _cnsPtr (a cog address), and the address of myncompr is copied to _cncomprPtr. You'll learn much more about this in the next chapter.

- **Lines 60–63**: Here the cog sits in a loop, continually copying the value of myns from its hub location (earlier, we copied @myns to _cnsPtr) to _cns. It checks whether myns is nonzero (which is the wz effect that you'll learn more about later); if it is still zero, it jumps back up to :mainLoop.

- **Lines 66–70**: The program arrives here if myns is nonzero, at which point we set myncompr to 3. This is done by setting _cncompr to 3 and then copying that value to hub memory. Then the program jumps back around to :mainLoop and repeats.

- **Lines 73–83**: Reserve space for some cog variables (I like to prepend the variable names with c to indicate they are local to the cog). I also have some temporary register variables (here r0).

OK, let's break this code down.

The CON section defines the codes for the compression. For example, if a difference value δ_j can be stored in 1 byte, then we write CODE08 in the comprCodeBuf (at the location corresponding to the j-th sample).

Pay particular attention to the VAR section where we have two long variables *one right after the other*.

```
long myns, myncompr
```

This means they are stored in consecutive locations in hub memory.

Next we have the INIT, START, and STOP methods. The START method has the following command:

```
ccogid := cognew(@STEIM, @myns)
```

This starts a new cog and returns the cog number if successful (or -1 if eight cogs are already running). To reiterate, the Propeller has eight independent processors or cogs. When you first run steim_pasm0_Demo, one cog starts up and runs all the code in MAIN. When MAIN calls COMPR. START, which runs cognew, a *new cog is launched.* The contents of this cog are the PASM instructions in the DAT section labeled STEIM (starting at line 53 and continuing to the FIT instruction at line 85). From this point forward, the STEIM cog is entirely independent (if you are coming from the C world, this is a fork and exec...). The only way for the MAIN cog and the STEIM cog to interact is for one of them to change variables in hub memory...and for the other cog to react to that change.

This means that each cog has to periodically check the same location in hub memory and has to include logic to decide that something must be done. Let's look at the parameter passing in more detail.

8.3 Passing Parameters in the cognew Command

The cognew command takes two arguments: the PASM cog to launch (@STEIM) and the address of a variable to share (here @myns).

```
ccogid := cognew (@STEIM, @myns)
```

When Spin encounters the command cognew, it does two things: it copies the PASM code into cog memory, *and* it places the value of the second argument to cognew (@myns—the memory location where the value myns lives) into the location PAR in cog memory. (PAR is always 0x1F0.) The STEIM cog can now get @myns from PAR, and using the rdlong and wrlong commands, it can read and change myns. The main cog (and other cogs) can also read and change myns, so there will need to be some protocol for making sure they don't collide. (In other words, if the STEIM cog reads myns and then writes a new value there some time later, we can't allow the main cog to mess with it during that time.)

An Analogy to PAR   Consider a train station—one of those lovely, high-ceiling Central European train stations filled with spies, intrigue, and good coffee. There is a room off to the side with rows of lockers (or at least back in the innocent days of my youth there were...). Each locker has a number. In this train station, there are only a few people: an elegant young woman with the odd name of Ms. Main Cog (main for short) and an older gentleman named Mr. Joe Steim (steim for short). They want to communicate, but they don't know what the other looks like.

When main wants to give steim a message, the only way she can do so is to place the message in a locker. steim can then open the locker and read and modify the message. main can come back some time later and re-open the locker and read what steim did. There is still a problem, though. main needs to tell steim which locker to open. This is where the information desk comes in (every train station has one, with some wonderfully patient, friendly, and knowledgeable folks). Before steim arrives (with the cognew command), main chooses a locker where she is going to leave messages and tells the lady at the information desk the locker number. When steim arrives, he goes to the information desk and asks "Did main leave a locker number for me?" *Voilà*. Both main and steim can now communicate.

The expression @myns is the address (the "locker number") of the variable myns. When passed to cognew, cognew places this address in a location known to everybody, called PAR (the "information desk" of my analogy).

8.3.1 Using PAR

The Spin code has this:

```
cognew(@STEIM, @myns)
```

The PASM cog has the statements shown in Listing 8-3.

Listing 8-3. PASM Fragment for Passing Parameters Using par

```
1  mov _cnsPtr, par
2  ...
3  _cnsPtr res 1
```

The mov _cnsPtr, par instruction copies the address stored in PAR (this is the "information desk" of my example) into the cog memory location _cnsPtr. The PASM cog also needs to reserve some space for that number, which it does with the _cnsPtr res 1 statement.

8.3.2 Using PAR Some More

In the Spin code, the variables myns and myncompr are declared thusly:

```
VAR
  long myns, myncompr
```

Therefore, we know that these two variables occupy successive memory in the hub. So, for example, if myns is at memory location 0x14, then myncompr will be at 0x18 (they are 4 bytes apart because they are longs). In Figure 8-1, the memory layout for the Hub and cog are shown.

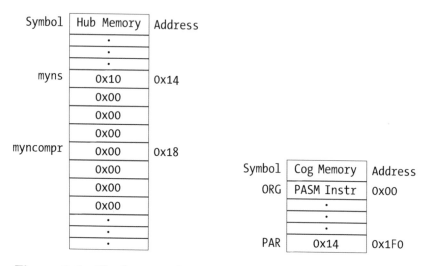

Figure 8-1. *The layout of Hub memory (left) and cog memory (right) showing how parameters are passing using the par register*

When cognew(@STEIM, @myns) is called, the Propeller places the number 0x14 (the address of myns) into memory location PAR. We use our knowledge about the layout of hub memory to now find out how to access myncompr.

```
  mov _cnsPtr, par
  mov _cncomprPtr, par
  add _cncomprPtr, #4
...
_cnsPtr res 1
_cncomprPtr res 1
```

The instruction mov _cnsPtr, par copies 0x14 into _cnsPtr. The instruction mov _cncomprPtr, par *also* copies 0x14 into _cncomprtPtr..., but the next instruction, add _cncomprPtr, #4, adds 4 to that value with the result of _cncomprPtr = 0x18, which is just what we want.

8.3.3 Using the Addresses

Now that we have those addresses for myns and myncompr, we can access the actual values.

```
rdlong _cns, _cnsPtr wz
...
mov _cncompr, #3
wrlong _cncompr, _cncomprPtr
```

There are only two sets of instructions to access hub memory: rdlong and wrlong (and their sisters rdbyte/wrbyte and rdword/wrword). The following instruction does two things:

```
rdlong _cns, _cnsPtr wz
```

It copies whatever is in the hub memory location that is *pointed to* by _cnsPtr into _cns. (Again, _cnsPtr contains the number 0x14; the rdlong instruction copies the long value that is stored at location 0x14 into the variable _cns.)

The second thing going on in that instruction is the wz *effect*. Every PASM instruction can have, as a side effect, the ability to change the flags Z and C. You have to read the manual to find out when and how Z and C are affected.

In the case of rdlong _cns, _cnsPtr wz, the Z flag is set to 1 (one) if the read operation results in a zero being written to _cns. If the read operation results in a nonzero value in _cns, then Z is set to 0 (zero). Read that paragraph a few times (and if it is unclear, drop us a line with suggestions!).

Now both cogs can do what they want with the variable myns.

8.3.4 Starting the Compression

The PASM cog continues after the instructions shown earlier and would continue to the end of cog memory except that we have some *branching* instructions.

```
:mainLoop
  rdlong _cns, _cnsPtr wz
  if_z jmp #:mainLoop
```

The expression :mainLoop is a *label*. It is a location that we can jump to. And we use that in this instruction:

```
if_z jmp #:mainLoop
```

The rdlong instruction sets Z according to whether _cns ends up being zero (in other words, whether myns in hub memory is zero or not). As long as myns is zero, then _cns will be zero, and therefore Z=1. The instruction if_z jmp #:mainLoop says that if Z==1, then jump to :mainLoop. If Z≠1, then continue to the next instruction. The reason for setting Z is so that we can make *branching* decisions based on whether myns is zero or not. As I said, the STEIM and main cogs are independent, and the way main asks STEIM to start a compression is by setting myns to the number of samples to compress (a nonzero value).

Once Ms. Main has asked Mr. Steim to start work (with the cognew command), he will periodically check the locker number 0x14 (named _cnsPtr in the PASM cog and myns in the main cog). If the note in there has the number zero on it, he will go back to cafe and get another espresso. If it has a nonzero number, then he knows he has work to do.

8.4 Passing Parameters: Method 2

The second way to pass parameters is to write a hub address to a cog variable *before* it is launched.

In the previous sections, we used the special memory location PAR to pass the address of a variable to the PASM cog.

To go back to Ms. Main and Mr. Steim passing messages in the train station, main launches steim with the cognew command. You can think of that action as if Mr. Steim were handed a book with 512 pages. He reads the instruction on page 0 and does as instructed; he moves on to page 1, and so on. Well, before you hand him the book, go to, for example, page 0x100 (oddly enough, both Ms. Main and Mr. Steim think in hex!) and write down the number of a locker that you want to share with him. Now both of you know the locker (and you don't have to get the information desk involved).

To review, the cognew command copies instructions, variables, reserved space, and special registers to a new cog (512 longs worth, of which the user has access to 496), as shown in Listing 8-4.

Listing 8-4. PASM Fragment Showing Cog Memory Layout

```
1  PUB START
2  ...
3    ccogid:= cognew(@STEIM, @myns)
4  ...
5
6  DAT 'pasm cog
7  STEIM ORG 0
8
```

```
 9  ... instructions
10    rdlong _cns, _cnsPtr wz
11
12  ... variables
13  _ccode24 long CODE24
14
15  ... reserved space
16  _cnsPtr res 1
17
18  FIT 496
19  ... system registers (PAR, CNT, etc)
```

For the cog to access a hub array such as logBuf, we will do the following:

1. We will define a new array in Spin called logBuf. (This is like deciding on a locker number.)

2. We will define a new variable in the PASM code called _clogBufPtr. (This is the "page number" 0x100 in the book of instructions that Mr. Steim is given.)

3. Before the cog is launched, we will place the address of logBuf into _clogBufPtr. (We write down the locker number on the correct page.)

We are, in effect, dynamically writing the PASM code, as shown in Listing 8-5.

Listing 8-5. PASM Fragment Showing Memory Layout for Passing Array Address in a Register

```
1  CON
2    LOGLEN = 256
3
4  VAR
```

```
 5    logBuf[LOGLEN]
 6
 7  PUB START
 8    _clogBufPtr := @logBuf
 9    ccogid := cognew(@STEIM, @myns)
10  ...
11
12  DAT 'pasm cog
13  STEIM ORG 0
14
15  ... instructions
16    rdlong _cns, _cnsPtr wz
17
18  ... variables
19  _ccode24 long CODE24
20
21  _clogBufPtr long 0
22
23  ... reserved space
24  _cnsPtr res 1
25
26  FIT 496
27  ... system registers (PAR, CNT, etc)
```

The instruction in the Spin code *just before* the cognew command, _clogBufPtr := @logBuf, is like writing down a locker number in the book. The layout of memory in Hub and cog are shown in Figure 8-2.

Symbol	Hub Memory	Address
	•	
	•	
	•	
logBuf[0]	0xnn	0x50
	0xnn	0x51
	0xnn	0x52
	0xnn	0x53
logBuf[1]	0xnn	0x54
	•	
	•	
	•	

Symbol	Cog Memory	Address
ORG	PASM Instr	0x00
	•	
	•	
	•	
_clogBufPtr	0x50	0x100
	•	
	•	
	•	

Figure 8-2. *The layout of memory in Hub and cog when we are passing parameters using an address written to a variable (method 2 of parameter-passing)*

Now both the Spin cog and the PASM cog can read and write from logBuf. The Spin cog can access logBuf[j] directly, and the PASM cog can access it using the rdlong/wrlong instructions to address _clogBufPtr. I will use this array in Chapter 11.

Naming Variables   The naming of variables should follow a pattern. Use a prefix for variables local to the cog followed by a short name for the variable (e.g., cns). Those variables that are addresses of variable ("locker numbers") should have Ptr appended (cnsPtr). I use c as a prefix for variables within the scope of the cog. This reduces the possibility of inadvertently using the wrong variable.

8.5 Summary

In this chapter, we looked at two different ways of passing data into and out of cogs. The first method is to place the address of a variable into the PAR register when a new cog is launched. The PASM cog can now read and write to that location (and to subsequent locations, if they also have variables of interest).

The second way is to store the address of a variable in a location that both the Spin and PASM code know about. This is done before the PASM cog is launched. There is no need to involve PAR in this case. See Listing 8-6 for a template for these two ways of passing parameters.

In Figure 8-3 we show an actual Information Desk at the old Penn Station in New York (sadly torn down in the 1960s).

Listing 8-6. A template for passing parameters from Spin to PASM cogs

```
1   VAR
2     'variable1 and variable2 are stored in successive locations
3     long variable1, variable2
4     ' this variable will be passed to the cog by storing
5     ' it 's value in a PASM variable BEFORE launch
6     long variable3
7
8   PUB MAIN
9     ' 1. cognew command will store the address of variable1
10    ' in PAR and then launch MYCOG in a new cog
11    ' 2. before we launch MYCOG, we place the address of ⏎
          variable3
```

```
12     ' into _cvariable3Ptr, which will be available to the cog
13     _cvariable3Ptr := @variable3
14     cognew(@MYCOG, @variable1)
15
16  DAT
17  MYCOG org 0
18     mov _cvar1Ptr, par ' when mycog is launched, ↵
                          ' par contains the ↵
19                        ' address of variable1
20     mov _cvar2Ptr, par ' the next long location ↵
                          ' contains the address
21     add _cvar2Ptr, #4 ' of variable2
22
23     rdlong _cvar1, _cvar1Ptr ' the actual value of variable1
24                             ' is obtained by a rdlong
25     rdlong _cvar2, _cvar2Ptr
26
27     rdlong _cvar3, _cvariable3Ptr ' _cvar3Ptr is populated ↵
                                     with the address
28                                   ' variable3 BEFORE launch, ↵
                                     so no need for par
29
30  _cvariable3Ptr long 0 ' variable where the address of ↵
                          variable3
31                        ' will be written BEFORE launch of cog
32  _cvar1Ptr res 1       ' space for the ptrs and vars that are
33  _cvar2Ptr res 1       ' passed thru par
34  _cvar1 res 1
35  _cvar2 res 1
36  _cvar3 res 1
```

Figure 8-3. *Information desk at the old Pennsylvania Station in New York.* `https://commons.wikimedia.org/wiki/File:Information_booth_at_the_Pennsylvania_railroad_station8d21848v.jpg.`

CHAPTER 9

Compression in PASM with TDD

Let's convert our Steim compressor to PASM using TDD. The specification in Chapter 5 is written for a "traditional" language where the compression routine is called by the main program (as in our Spin example). As we want to implement the compression routine in PASM, we will start a new cog and will have to perform *handshaking*, as it is called, between the two cogs as follows (Figure 9-1):

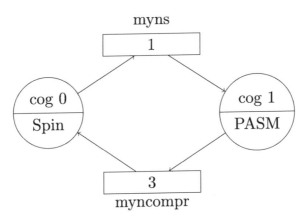

Figure 9-1. *Diagram showing the handshaking between the Spin cog and the PASM cog*

© Sridhar Anandakrishnan 2018
S. Anandakrishnan, *Propeller Programming*, https://doi.org/10.1007/978-1-4842-3354-2_9

As shown in Figure 9-1, the main Spin cog will set myns to a nonzero value, which will trigger the PASM cog to perform the compression. When the PASM cog finishes its work, it will set myncompr to a nonzero value, which signals the main cog that the compression is complete.

Let's look at the "file view" and "cog view" of the project. The Spin code is split between the main file (steim_pasm_Demo) and the actual compressor file (steim_pasm), shown in Figure 9-2. The main file and the compressor file are related as shown in Figure 9-2: the main or driver file includes the worker file using the OBJ keyword.

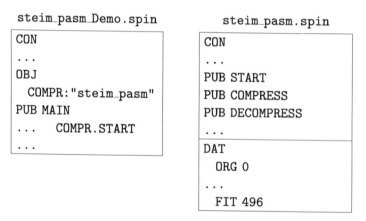

Figure 9-2. *The file-level view of the compression program, with the driver file on the left and the worker file on the right*

The cog view of the project is (in part) as follows: cog0 runs main and the Spin methods in steim_pasm. cog1 runs the PASM code for the compression and decompression (Figure 9-3). The PASM code is triggered by changes in hub memory (when myns is set to a nonzero value).

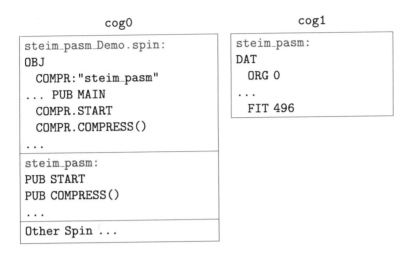

cog0

```
steim_pasm_Demo.spin:
OBJ
  COMPR:"steim_pasm"
... PUB MAIN
  COMPR.START
  COMPR.COMPRESS()
...
```
```
steim_pasm:
PUB START
PUB COMPRESS()
...
```
```
Other Spin ...
```

cog1

```
steim_pasm:
DAT
  ORG 0
...
  FIT 496
```

Figure 9-3. *The cog-level view of the compression program*

The files for this program are on GitHub.

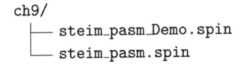

```
ch9/
    ├── steim_pasm_Demo.spin
    └── steim_pasm.spin
```

9.1 Overall Flowchart

Figure 9-4 shows the flowchart for the PASM cog. When $N > 0$ (myns), the cog will read and process a sample. Every 16th sample, it will write out a compression code long. Upon completion, it will write out the last compression code long. It will set $N = 0$ and write out the number of bytes used in the compression, N_c (myncompr).

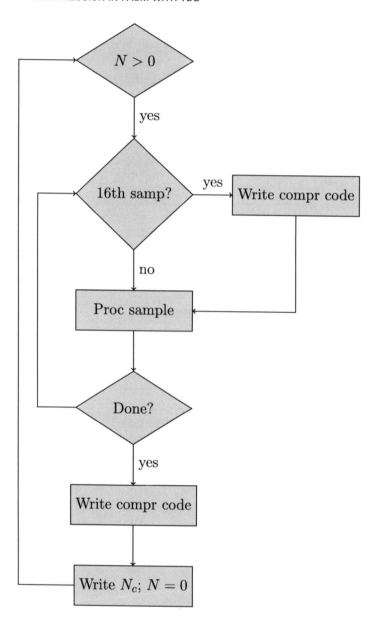

Figure 9-4. *Flowchart for compression of samples*

9.2 Test 1: Passing nsamps and ncompr

Let's write a test for a small part of this: setting myncompr to non-negative.
The test will do the following:

1. The calling cog (main) will set the number of
   samples (myns in the COMPR object) to the number of
   samples in sampsBuf.

2. Upon completion of compression, the STEIM PASM
   cog will set the number of compressed bytes
   (myncompr) to a non-negative number.

9.2.1 Spin Code

Listing 9-1 shows the Spin code. Add it to main.

Listing 9-1. Spin Code

```
1   PUB MAIN
2   ...
3
4     TEST_THAT_NCOMPR_IS_SET_TO_NONNEGATIVE
5
6   ...
7   PUB TEST_THAT_NCOMPR_IS_SET_TO_NONNEGATIVE | nc, t0
8   " test methods are rarely commented - the name should be
9   " explanatory ...
10    nsamps := 1
11    nc := COMPR.COMPRESS (@sampsBuf, nsamps, @packBuf, ⮐
      @comprCodeBuf)
12    t0 := nc => 0
13    TDD.ASSERT_TRUTHY (t0, string("Test that the compression ⮐
      cog sets ncompr => 0"))
```

The test is relatively simple. The test method in main sets nsamps to 1 and calls COMPR.COMPRESS. Within the COMPRESS object, myns is set to 1, which triggers the compression.

9.2.2 PASM Code

Listing 9-2 shows the START code that launches the PASM cog, the COMPRESS code, and the PASM code from the previous chapter with the *handshaking* discussed in detail.

Listing 9-2. PASM Code

```
1   ...
2   PUB START
3       STOP
4   '   myns <> 0 controls when the compression is started
5       myns := 0
6       ccogid := cognew(@STEIM, @myns)
7       return ccogid
8
9   PUB COMPRESS(psampsBuf, ns, ...)
10  ...
11    myns := 0
12    myncompr := 0
13
14    ' this will start the compression
15    myns := ns
16
17    ' when ncompr is non -zero, the compression is complete
18    repeat until myncompr > 0
19    return myncompr
```

```
20  ...
21
22  STEIM org 0
23    ' copy the param addresses
24    mov _cnsPtr, par
25    mov _cncomprPtr, par
26    add _cncomprPtr, #4
27
28  : mainLoop
29    ' the signal for starting the compression is when ns <> 0
30    rdlong _cns, _cnsPtr wz
31    if_z jmp #:mainLoop
32
33    ' set myns to zero first so we don't start another ↵
      cycle ...
34    mov _cns, #0
35    wrlong _cns, _cnsPtr
36
37    ' signal completion
38    mov _cncompr, #3
39    wrlong _cncompr, _cncomprPtr
40
41    ' wait for another compression request
42    jmp #:mainLoop
```

The START function is called once by the driver file, and that starts the
PASM cog. The COMPRESS function can be called any number of times, and
it communicates with the (running) PASM cog via the value of myns. When
the COMPRESS function sets myns := ns, that sets myns to 1. The running
PASM cog is continually monitoring myns (via the rdlong in the steim cog
that sets _cns). Because of the wz effect of the rdlong, the instruction will

set Z to 0 when _cns is nonzero. Now, instead of jumping back around to :mainLoop, control will pass to the next instructions:

```
' set myns to zero first so we don't start another cycle...
mov _cns, #0
wrlong _cns, _cnsPtr
mov _cncompr, #3
wrlong _cncompr, _cncomprPtr
' wait for another compression request
jmp #:mainLoop
```

Next, we set _cns to zero and write that back to hub memory (to myns) so that when we go back up to :mainLoop, we don't immediately start another compression cycle. Finally, we set the variable _cncompr to 3 and then write that value to hub memory (to myncompr) with the wrlong instruction.

In the Spin code in COMPRESS, the following statement will loop at that line continuously until myncompr is greater than zero, which it will be soon, when the PASM code does its wrlong!

```
repeat until myncompr > 0
```

At that point, the Spin code will continue to the next instruction.

```
return myncompr
```

Back in the calling function, nc will be set to 3, the value t0 will be true, and the ASSERT_TRUTHY call will print OK.

```
nc := COMPR.COMPRESS(@sampsBuf, nsamps, @packBuf,
@comprCodeBuf)
t0 := nc => 0
```

9.3 Test 2: Packing Sample 0

In the previous section, we passed nsamps to the steim cog, which signals the start of the compression process. In this section, we will actually compress sample 0 and populate packBuf and comprCodeBuf. If you recall from the specification and from the Spin code examples, the three low bytes of sampsBuf[0] are placed in packBuf, and the code for a 3-byte compression is placed in the low 2 bits of comprCodeBuf[0].

9.3.1 Spin Code

To read from sampsBuf and write to the other two arrays, we need to pass their addresses to the steim cog. Listing 9-3 shows the modified calling routine, with three new tests that check whether sample 0 is packed correctly, whether ncompr is set correctly (to 3), and whether comprCodeBuf[0] is set correctly to COMPR.CODE24.

Listing 9-3. Driver File Testing Code

```
1   PUB MAIN
2   ...
3
4     TEST_THAT_SAMP0_IS_PACKED_PROPERLY
5     TEST_THAT_SAMP0_SETS_NCOMPR_TO_3
6     TEST_THAT_SAMP0_SETS_COMPRCODE_TO_CODE24
7
8   ...
9   PUB TEST_THAT_SAMP0_IS_PACKED_PROPERLY | t0, nc
10    sampsBuf[0] := $AB_CD_EF
11    nsamps := 1
```

```
12    nc := COMPR.COMPRESS (@sampsBuf, nsamps, @packBuf, ↵
      @comprCodeBuf)
13    t0 := (packBuf[0] == sampsBuf[0] & $FF)
14    t0 &= (packBuf[1] == sampsBuf[0] >> 8 & $FF)
15    t0 &= (packBuf[2] == sampsBuf[0] >> 16 & $FF)
16    TDD.ASSERT_TRUTHY(t0, string(" Test that samp0 is packed ↵
      correctly into packbuf "))
17
18  PUB TEST_THAT_SAMP0_SETS_NCOMPR_TO_3 | t0, nc
19    sampsBuf[0] := $AB_CD_EF
20    nsamps := 1
21    nc := COMPR.COMPRESS (@sampsBuf, nsamps, @packBuf, ↵
      @comprCodeBuf )
22    t0 := nc == 3
23    TDD.ASSERT_TRUTHY(t0, string("Test that samp0 sets ↵
      ncompr =3"))
24
25  PUB TEST_THAT_SAMP0_SETS_COMPRCODE_TO_CODE24 | t0
26    sampsBuf[0] := $AB_CD_EF
27    nsamps := 1
28    nc := COMPR.COMPRESS (@sampsBuf, nsamps, @packBuf, ↵
      @comprCodeBuf)
29    t0 := comprCodeBuf[0] == COMPR#CODE24
30    TDD.ASSERT_TRUTHY(t0, string("Test that samp0 sets ↵
      comprCodeBuf to CODE24"))
```

9.3.2 Memory Layout of Arrays and Parameters

As in the previous section, we now need to pass the addresses of sampsBuf, packBuf, and comprCodeBuf as well to the steim cog.

Modify the VAR declaration for myns and myncompr to now include three new variables: sampsBufAddr, packBufAddr, and comprCodeBufAddr. These variables are all listed one after the other, so they occupy successive long locations.

There is one crucial difference, however, between myns and sampsBufAddr: the number stored at location @myns/0x14 is the *actual value of myns* (1). The number stored at sampsBufAddr/0x1C is *the address of the location* where sampsBuf lives in hub memory; here I have put in some arbitrary number as an example (0x104). In Figure 9-5, I show the layout of hub memory with the longs following @myns (myncompr, sampsBufAddr, etc.). The array sampsBuf itself is in a different part of memory, but its address is in sampsBufAddr, which will be made available to the PASM cog. You need to do this "indirect addressing" when you want to pass the address of an array that is stored elsewhere.

Symbol	HUB Memory	Address
myns	0x01	0x14
myncompr	0x00	0x18
sampsBufAddr	0x104	0x1C
packBufAddr	0x472	0x20
comprCodeBufAddr	0x400	0x24
	·	
	·	
	·	
sampsBuf	0xEF	0x104
	0xCD	0x105
	0xAB	0x106
	0x00	0x107

Figure 9-5. *Memory layout in hub showing the arrangement of variables that will be passed to the PASM cog. sampsBufAddr contains the address to the first sample of sampsBuf, which is shown further along in memory.*

The COMPRESS method gets those values because the calling routine passes @sampsBuf (the address of sampsBuf), and this is similar for the other two arrays.

Those three addresses are stored in the variables sampsBufAddr, packBufAddr, and comprCodeBufAddr, and when myns is set to nonzero, the steim cog will start the compression, using those addresses.

```
VAR
  long myns, myncompr, sampsBufAddr, packBufAddr,
comprCodeBufAddr

PUB COMPRESS(psampsBuf, ns, ppackBuf, pcomprCodeBuf) : ncompr
  sampsBufAddr := psampsBuf
  packBufAddr := ppackBuf
  comprCodeBufAddr := pcomprCodeBuf
  ' this will start the compression
  myns := ns
```

9.3.3 PASM Code

In the PASM code, we have already looked at how to access myns; now let's look at how to access sampsBuf[0] using *indirect addressing* (Listing 9-4).

Listing 9-4. Indirect Addressing in PASM to Read from an Array

```
1  ...
2  : mainLoop
3    ' the signal for starting the compression is when ns <> 0
4    rdlong _cns, _cnsPtr wz
5    if_z jmp #:mainLoop
6
7    ' get the array start addresses
8    mov r0, par
9    add r0, #8
```

```
10      rdlong _csampsbufPtr, r0
11
12      mov r0, par
13      add r0, #12
14      rdlong _cpackbufPtr, r0
15
16      mov r0, par
17      add r0, #16
18      rdlong _ccomprcodebufPtr, r0
19
20      call #GET_SAMPLE
21      call #HANDLE_SAMP0
22
23      ' set myns to zero first so we don't start another ↵
        cycle ...
24      mov _cns, #0
25      wrlong _cns, _cnsPtr
26      ' signal completion
27      wrlong _cncompr, _cncomprPtr
```

- **Lines 8–9**: Copy the contents of PAR (the address of myns) to a temporary variable r0 and add 8 to it. Now r0 will have the address of the *location that has the address* of sampsBuf (0x1C).

- **Line 10**: The rdlong gets that address so that _csampsBufPtr is set to 0x104 (the address of the sampsBuf array in the hub).

We then copy the contents of the long at 0x1C to csampsbufPtr: csampsbufPtr = 0x104. We now have the location of sampsBuf[0]. We go through a similar procedure for the other two arrays, packBuf and comprCodeBuf.

175

9.3.4 Subroutines in PASM

As in other languages, you can define a subroutine when there is code that is often repeated or simply to keep your code modular and organized. In this case, I define two subroutines: GET_SAMPLE and HANDLE_SAMP0.

Subroutines are defined by enclosing them between two labels: SUBROUTINE_NAME and SUBROUTINE_NAME_ret. In addition, the second label (SUBROUTINE_NAME_ret) should be immediately followed by the PASM instruction ret. There are no formal arguments or parameters for the subroutine. Rather, the subroutine is in the same scope as the calling code. All variables are available and can be read and modified. Therefore, it is important to be clear on which variables are needed by the subroutine and which are modified. In Listing 9-5, I show the GET_SAMPLE and HANDLE_SAMP0 subroutines. The comments at the start show which variables are read and which are modified.

Listing 9-5. Examples of subroutines, with comments showing variables that are used and modified

```
1   GET_SAMPLE
2   "  read a sample from sampsBuf
3   "  modifies samp
4   "  increments sampsbufPtr to next sample
5      rdlong _csamp, _csampsbufPtr
6      add _csampsbufPtr, #4
7   GET_SAMPLE_ret ret
8
9   HANDLE_SAMP0
10  "  write the three bytes of samp to packbuf
11  "  write code24 to comprcodebuf [0]
12  "  destroys samp
13  "  modifies ncompr
14
```

```
15    mov r0, #3
16  :s0loop
17      wrbyte _csamp, _cpackbufPtr
18      add _cpackbufPtr, #1
19      shr _csamp, #8
20      djnz r0, #:s0loop
21      ' loop terminates here
22      mov _cncompr, #3
23      mov _ccomprcode, _ccode24
24      wrlong _ccomprcode, _ccomprcodebufPtr
25  HANDLE_SAMP0_ret ret
```

GET_SAMPLE is straightforward. It reads a long from the *current index* of sampBuf (initially 0) and increments the index to point at the next value in sampsBuf.

HANDLE_ SAMP0 takes that sample and writes the low 3 bytes back to packBuf. The following sequence is like a repeat 3 in Spin or a for loop in C. Set r0 to the number of times you want to loop and, at the end of the loop, decrement it by 1 and test for when it is equal to 0 (djnz r0, #:s0loop says "decrement r0 and jump to s0loop if r0 is not zero"). After three times, the loop terminates, and the instructions following djnz are executed.

```
  mov r0, #3
:s0loop
  <<do something>>
  djnz r0, #:s0loop
<<here after 3 iteration>>
```

The "do something" part is where the 3 bytes of sampsBuf[0] are copied to packBuf. The instruction wrbyte _csamp, _cpackbufPtr will copy the lowest byte of_csamp to the current address in_cpackbufPtr. The next instruction, add _cpackbufPtr, #1, will add the *literal value* 1 to the address _cpackbufPtr. This increments the index of packBuf. The next and final instruction in the loop, shr _csamp, #8, shifts the contents of the variable _csamp right by 8 bits (in other words, shifts the low byte out and moves the next higher byte into the low byte position). Finally, the instruction djnz r0, #:s0loop will decrement r0 by 1 and loop to :s0loop if r0≠0.

The first time through the loop, the low byte (bits 0–7) of _csamp is copied to packBuf[0]. The second time (after the increment of _cpackbufPtr and the shift right by 8 bits of _csamp), the second byte (the original bits 8–15 of _csamp) is copied to packBuf[1]. The third time, the third byte of _csamp is copied to packBuf[2]. In the process, _csamp is destroyed—and we note that in the comments for the subroutine so that the calling routine knows not to use _csamp again.

9.3.5 Testing the Compression of Sample 0

Let's run our tests (including running our previous test). If these succeed, we are confident that the array addresses are being passed correctly.

```
Compression
mainCogId:      0
comprCogId:     2
Test that the compression cog sets ncompr => 0
...ok
Test that sample 0 is properly packed to packBuf
...ok
Test that compressor sets ncompr correctly for sample 0
...ok
Test that compressor sets compression code correctly for sample 0
...ok
Tests Run: 4
Tests  Passed:  4
Tests Failed: 0
```

9.4 Packing Differences for Latter Samples

Now that we know how to access the arrays, we can proceed with compressing all the samples by forming differences and packing those differences in packBuf based on their length.

Here is the PASM code in Listing 9-6. Here we add code to handle all the samples and to set the compression codes correctly.

Listing 9-6. Changes to the PASM code to handle all the samples and to set the compression codes correctly

```
1      ...
2      mov r0, par
3      add r0, #16
4      rdlong _ccomprcodebufPtr, r0
5
6      mov _cj, #0 ' j-th samp
7      ' there are 16 codes in each code word
8      ' there are NSAMPS_LONG /16 code longs (e.g., 8 ↵
       codelongs for 128 samps)
9      ' samps 0-15 have their codes in _ccodebufptr [0],
10     ' samps 16 -31 have their codes in _ccodebufptr [1], etc
11     ' _ccodebitidx is the location within a long (0, 2, 4, ↵
       ... 30)
12     ' _ccodelongidx is the idx of the long in the code array
13     mov _ccodebitidx, #0
14     mov _ccodelongidx, #0
15
16     call #GET_SAMPLE
17     mov _cprev, _csamp ' save sample for diff
18     call #HANDLE_SAMP0
19     add _ccodebitidx, #2
20
21     sub _cns, #1 wz
22     if_z jmp #:done
23
```

179

```
24  : loopns
25     call #GET_SAMPLE
26     call #HANDLE_SAMPJ
27     mov _cprev, _csamp
28     add _cj, #1
29
30     add _ccodebitidx, #2
31     test _ccodebitidx, #31 wz
32     if_nz jmp #:samelong
33
34     wrlong _ccomprcode, _ccomprcodebufptr
35     add _ccomprcodebufptr, #4
36     mov _ccomprcode, #0
37
38  : samelong
39     djnz _cns, #:loopns
40
41  :done
42     ' wait for another compression request - zero out myns
43     ' so we don't immediately start another compression cycle
44     wrlong _cns, _cnsPtr
45     ' signal completion
46     wrlong _cncompr, _cncomprPtr
47     jmp #:mainLoop
48  ...
49  HANDLE_SAMPJ
50  " form difference between j and j-1 samps
51  " determine byte - length of diff
52  " save diff to packbuf
53  " increment ncompr appropriately
```

```
54  " modify comprcode appropriately

55

56  HANDLE_SAMPJ_ret ret
```

We have added these variables:

- _cj: The current sample number.

- _ccodelongidx: The index into the array comprCodeBuf where the current sample's code will be stored.

- _ccodebitidx: The bit location within the long where the code will be stored.

- _cprev and _cdiff: The previous sample and the difference between the current and previous samples.

After initializing these variables (lines 6–14), we handle the special case of sample 0 (lines 16–18). Here we add the instruction mov _cprev, _csamp before the subroutine call HANDLE_SAMP0. Remember, that subroutine destroys _csamp, so if we want to use it to form the difference, we must save it. Next, we check for whether there is only one sample, and if so, we are done (lines 20–21): subtract 1 from _cns (the number of samples) and set the Z flag if the result is 0 (that is the effect of wz). If Z is set, jump to the code to finalize the compression (done) when the myncompr variables in hub memory are set to the correct values (which signals the main cog that the compression has completed).

If there is more than one sample to process, continue and process those samples in lines 23–38.

- **Lines 24–25**: Get the next sample and process it (we'll look at HANDLE_SAMPJ in a moment).

- **Lines 26–27**: Save the sample for the next loop and increment j.

- **Lines 29–31**: The bit index moves up by 2, and we check whether we need to move to the next comprCodeBuf long. The instruction test_ccodebitidx, #31 wz will set Z if ccodebitidx is equal to 32 (31=%0001 1111 and 32=%0010 0000; the bitwise AND of the two numbers is 0, which will set Z to 1) The instruction test is like and, but doesn't save the result; it only affects the flags. If Z is not set, then we are still within this comprCodeBuf long, and we jump around the subsequent code.

- **Lines 33–35**: New comprCodeBuf long. Write the completed long to hub memory and increment the pointer to point to the next long.

OK, now let's look at HANDLE_SAMPJ, shown in Listing 9-7. Here we take the difference between the two samples and determine if that number would fit in one, two, or three bytes and handle packBuf and comprCodeBuf accordingly.

Listing 9-7. Subroutine to form the difference between two samples and to update packBuf and comprCodeBuf depending on the size of the difference

```
1   HANDLE_SAMPJ
2   " form the difference diff=csamp -cprev
3   " if |diff| < 127, write 1 byte of diff
4   " if |diff| < 32767, write 2 bytes of diff
5   " else write three bytes of diff.
6   " ccode, ccodebitidx changed
7   " packbufptr incremented by 1,2, or 3
8
9     mov _cdiff, _csamp
10    sub _cdiff, _cprev
11
12    ' write a byte and check if more need to be written
```

```
13    ' repeat as necessary
14    ' r0 - running count of number of bytes used by diff
15    ' r1 - compr code - updated as more bytes are used
16    ' r2 - abs value of cdiff
17    wrbyte _cdiff, _cpackBufptr
18    add _cpackBufptr, #1
19    mov r0, #1
20    mov r1, _ccode08
21    ' is -127 < cdiff < 127
22    abs r2, _cdiff
23    cmp r2, _onebyte wc,wz
24    if_c_or_z jmp #:donej
25
26    ' write 2nd byte
27    shr _cdiff, #8
28    wrbyte _cdiff, _cpackBufptr
29    add _cpackBufptr, #1
30    add r0, #1
31    mov r1, _ccode16
32    ' is -32K < cdiff < 32k
33    cmp r2, _twobyte wc,wz
34    if_c_or_z jmp #:donej
35
36    ' must be 3 bytes long ...
37    shr _cdiff, #8
38    wrbyte _cdiff, _cpackBufptr
39    add _cpackBufptr, #1
40    add r0, #1
41    mov r1, _ccode24
42
43  :donej
44    add _cncompr, r0 ' add number of bytes seen here to ncompr
45    rol r1, _ccodebitidx
46    or _ccode, r1
47
48  HANDLE_SAMPJ_ret ret
49  ...
```

```
50  _onebyte long $7F
51  _twobyte long $7F_FF
```

- **Lines 9–10**: Form the difference `diff = samp - prev`.

- **Lines 17–24**: Write the low byte of `diff` to `packBuf` and set the code temporarily to CODE08. Check if $\|\delta_j\| < 127$: `cmp r2, _onebyte wc,wz`. The constant `_onebyte` is 127, and `wz` says to set Z if r2 is equal to 127; `wc` says to set C if r2 is less than 127. `if_c_or_z jmp #:donej` says to jump to `donej` if C or Z is set.

- **Lines 26–41**: If r2 is greater than 127, then write the second byte of `diff`; check again if that is all we need to do. If not, write the third byte of `diff`.

- **Lines 43–46**: r0 has the number of bytes of diff (1, 2, or 3). Add it to `_cncompr`. r1 has the compression code (CODE08, CODE16, or CODE24). Shift it to the correct location (`rol` means "rotate left") and set those two bits of `_ccode` (with an `or` instruction).

9.4.1 Testing Compressing Two Samples!

The following are the tests for the new code to test the code for compression (Listing 9-8). Hopefully the names of the methods and the informational string (in TDD.ASSERT_TRUTHY) are self-explanatory. Each testing method tests a small piece of functionality and should be re-run whenever changes are made to the code.

Listing 9-8. Some of the tests that exercise different parts of the compression code

```
1   PUB MAIN
2   ...
3     TEST_THAT_SAMP1_IS_PROPERLY_PACKED_ONE_BYTE
4     TEST_THAT_SAMP1_IS_PROPERLY_PACKED_TWO_BYTES
5     TEST_THAT_SAMP1_IS_PROPERLY_PACKED_THREE_BYTES
6     TEST_THAT_SAMP1_SETS_COMPRCODE_CORRECTLY
7     TEST_THAT_SAMP1_SETS_COMPRCODE_CORRECTLY_TWO_BYTES
8   ...
9   PRI TEST_THAT_SAMP1_IS_PROPERLY_PACKED_ONE_BYTE | t0, nc, d
10    nsamps := 2
11    d := 42
12    sampsBuf[0] := $AB_CD_EF
13    sampsBuf[1] := sampsBuf[0] + d ' diff will be < 127
14    nc := COMPR.COMPRESS (@sampsBuf, nsamps, @packBuf, ↩
      @comprCodeBuf)
15    t0 := nc <> -1 & (packBuf[3] == d)
16    TDD.ASSERT_TRUTHY (t0, string("Test that sample 1 is ↩
      properly packed to packBuf (1 byte)"))
17
18  PRI TEST_THAT_SAMP1_IS_PROPERLY_PACKED_TWO_BYTES | t0, nc,d
19    nsamps := 2
20    d := 314
21    sampsBuf[0] := $AB_CD_EF
22    sampsBuf[1] := sampsBuf[0] + d ' diff will be less < 32k ↩
      but > 127
23    nc :=COMPR.COMPRESS (@sampsBuf, nsamps, @packBuf, ↩
      @comprCodeBuf)
24    t0 := nc <> -1 & (packBuf [3] == d & $FF) & (packBuf [4] ↩
      == d >> 8 & $FF)
```

```
25    TDD.ASSERT_TRUTHY (t0, string("Test that sample 1 is ↵
      properly packed to packBuf (two bytes)"))
26
27  PRI TEST_THAT_SAMP1_SETS_COMPRCODE_CORRECTLY | t0, nc
28    nsamps := 2
29    sampsBuf[0] := $AB_CD_EF
30    sampsBuf[1] := $AB_CD_EF + $42
31    nc := COMPR.COMPRESS (@sampsBuf, nsamps, @packBuf, ↵
      @comprCodeBuf)
32    t0 := nc <> -1 & (comprCodeBuf [1] & %1111 ==
      (COMPR#CODE08 <<2) | (COMPR # CODE24))
33    TDD.ASSERT_TRUTHY (t0, string("Test that compressor sets ↵
      compression code correctly for sample 1"))
34
35  PRI TEST_THAT_SAMP1_SETS_COMPRCODE_CORRECTLY_TWO_BYTES | t0, nc
36    nsamps := 2
37    sampsBuf[0] := $AB_CD_EF
38    sampsBuf[1] := $AB_CD_EF + $42_42
39    nc :=COMPR.COMPRESS (@sampsBuf, nsamps, @packBuf, ↵
      @comprCodeBuf)
40    t0 := nc <> -1 & (comprCodeBuf [1] & %1111 == (COMPR# ↵
      CODE16 << 2) | (COMPR # CODE24))
41    TDD.ASSERT_TRUTHY (t0, string("Test that compressor sets ↵
      compression code correctly for sample 1 (2 bytes)"))
```

```
Compression
mainCogId: 0
comprCogId: 2
Test that the compression cog sets ncompr => 0
...ok
Test that sample 0 is properly packed to packBuf
...ok
```

```
Test that compressor sets ncompr correctly for sample 0
...ok
Test that compressor sets compression code correctly for sample 0
...ok
Test that sample 1 is properly packed to packBuf (1 byte)
...ok
Test that sample 1 is properly packed to packBuf (two bytes)
...ok
Test that compressor sets compression code correctly for sample 1
...ok
Test that compressor sets compression code correctly for sample 1 ↵
(2 bytes)
...ok

Tests Run: 8
Tests Passed: 8
Tests Failed: 0
```

9.4.2 Test Compressing an Arbitrary Number of Samples

Now that we have tested the cases of two samples being packed
correctly, let's see if an arbitrary number of samples are packed correctly.
Remember, the compression codes are written two bits at a time; the
compression codes for samples 0–15 are stored in comprCodeBuf[0] and
for sample 16 into comprCodeBuf[1]. We need to exercise the code in as
many "edge" cases as possible. Here are the most basic ones: 16 samples,
17 samples, and 127 samples. This is not an exhaustive test but will give
us some confidence that we are packing the bytes correctly and writing
the compression codes correctly. Now that we know that the first and

second sample are handled correctly, let's write tests that walk through compressing the whole array, including testing for "edge cases" where problems often occur (Listing 9-9).

Listing 9-9. Testing that more than two samples can be compressed correctly

```
1   PUB MAIN
2   ...
3     TEST_THAT_SAMP15_PACKS_PROPERLY
4     TEST_THAT_SAMP16_PACKS_PROPERLY
5     TEST_THAT_SAMP127_PACKS_PROPERLY
6   ...
7   PRI TEST_THAT_SAMP15_PACKS_PROPERLY | t0, nc, i, d
8     nsamps := 16
9     longfill(@sampsBuf, 0, 16)
10
11    sampsBuf[14] := 12
12    d := -42
13    sampsBuf[15] := 12 + d
14    nc := COMPR.COMPRESS (@sampsBuf, nsamps, @packBuf, ↵
      @comprCodeBuf)
15    repeat i from 0 to nc -1
16      UARTS.HEX(DEBUG, packBuf [i], 2)
17      UARTS.PUTC(DEBUG, SPACE)
18
19    t0 := nc == 18
20    TDD.ASSERT_TRUTHY (t0, string("Test that compressor ↵
      sets nc correctly for samp 15"))
21    t0 := comprCodeBuf[0] >> 30 == %01
22    TDD.ASSERT_TRUTHY (t0, string("Test that compressor ↵
      sets compr code correctly for samp 15"))
23    t0 := packBuf [nc -1] == d & $FF
```

```
24    TDD.ASSERT_TRUTHY (t0, string("Test that compressor ↵
      sets compr code correctly for samp 15"))
25
26  PRI TEST_THAT_SAMP16_PACKS_PROPERLY | t0, nc, i, d
27    nsamps := 17
28    longfill(@sampsBuf, 0, 17)
29
30    sampsBuf[15] := 12
31    d := -42
32    sampsBuf[16] := 12 + d
33    nc := COMPR.COMPRESS (@sampsBuf, nsamps, @packBuf, ↵
      @comprCodeBuf)
34    t0 := nc == 19
35    TDD.ASSERT_TRUTHY (t0, string("Test that compressor sets ↵
      nc correctly for samp 16"))
36    t0 := comprCodeBuf[1] & %11 == %01 '
37    TDD.ASSERT_TRUTHY (t0, string("Test that compressor sets ↵
      compr code correctly for samp 16"))
38    t0 := packBuf [nc -1] == d & $FF
39    TDD.ASSERT_TRUTHY (t0, string("Test that compressor sets ↵
      compr code correctly for samp 16"))
40
41  PRI TEST_THAT_SAMP127_PACKS_PROPERLY | t0, nc, i, d
42    nsamps := 128
43    longfill(@sampsBuf, 0, 128)
44
45    sampsBuf[126] := 12
46    d := -42
47    sampsBuf[127] := 12 + d
48    nc := COMPR.COMPRESS (@sampsBuf, nsamps, @packBuf, ↵
      @comprCodeBuf )
49    t0 := nc == 130
```

```
50    TDD.ASSERT_TRUTHY (t0, string("Test that compressor sets ↵
      nc correctly for samp 127"))
51    t0 := comprCodeBuf[7] >> 30 == %01 '
52    TDD.ASSERT_TRUTHY (t0, string("Test that compressor sets ↵
      compr code correctly for samp 127"))
53    t0 := packBuf [nc -1] == d & $FF
54    TDD.ASSERT_TRUTHY (t0, string("Test that compressor sets ↵
      compr code correctly for samp 127"))
```

In all these tests, we zero out sampsBuf and then set the last two samples to known values. We run the compression and make sure the number of compressed bytes is correct and that the packed array and compression code array have the correct values.

9.5 Success?

Did we speed things up? By how much?

```
nc= 382
dt= 29264
dt (ms) ~ 0
```

The Spin version took 1.5 million clocks, and the PASM version takes 29,000 clocks. This is *a factor of 50 speedup*. (Our original estimate was for 25,000 clocks in the PASM version, so that's not bad.)

Let's do a more comprehensive set of tests by writing a decompressor in the next chapter.

9.6 Summary

In this chapter, we showed how to pass an array to a PASM cog. When a new cog is launched, the address (in the hub) of a variable can be stored in the PAR register, which the new cog can use. To pass arrays, we need another level of indirection! The address at the start of the array is stored in a memory location. The address of that memory location is passed to the PASM cog in PAR (Listing 9-10 has a template that you can modify for new programs). PASM requires that we pay attention to every detail of the computation and build the "scaffolding" of our program from the ground up, much as is shown in Figure 9-6 for a railroad bridge used by Union Army during the Civil War.

Listing 9-10. Template for passing parameters to a PASM cog that uses both methods discussed in this chapter

```
1   VAR
2      long dataArray[100]
3      long dataArrayPtr
4
5   PUB MAIN
6      ' store the address of start of dataArray in dataArrayPtr
7      dataArrayPtr := @dataArray
8      ' pass the address of dataArrayPtr to the new cog in PAR
9      cognew(@MYARRCOG, @dataArrayPtr)
10
11  DAT
12  MYARRCOG org 0
13     ' par has the address of dataArrayPtr, which is copied to r0
14     mov r0, par
15     ' doing a rdlong from that address gets the address of ↵
       the start
```

191

```
16    ' of dataArray
17    rdlong _cdataArrPtr, r0
18
19    ' doing a rdlong from _cdataArrPtr gets the first element ⏎
      of dataArray
20    rdlong _cdata, _cdataArrPtr
21    ...
22    ' increment to the next element of dataArray and get it ...
23    add _cdataArrPtr, #4
24    rdlong _cdata, _dataArrPtr
```

Figure 9-6. *Railroad bridge across Potomac Creek, 1863 or 1864. "That man Haupt has built a bridge across Potomac Creek, about 400 feet long and nearly 100 feet high, over which loaded trains are running every hour and, upon my word, gentlemen, there is nothing in it but beanpoles and cornstalks!" —Abraham Lincoln, May 23, 1862. Library of Congress, ppmsca.11749.*

CHAPTER 10

Decompression in PASM

In this chapter we will write a PASM decompressor. We will go in the opposite direction from the compression code (flowchart in Figure 10-1): converting the packBuf array to the sampsBuf array (using the comprCodeBuf array to help in the reconstruction). In Figure 10-2, we have a great picture demonstrating that what goes up must come down... and that work can be fun!

© Sridhar Anandakrishnan 2018
S. Anandakrishnan, *Propeller Programming*, https://doi.org/10.1007/978-1-4842-3354-2_10

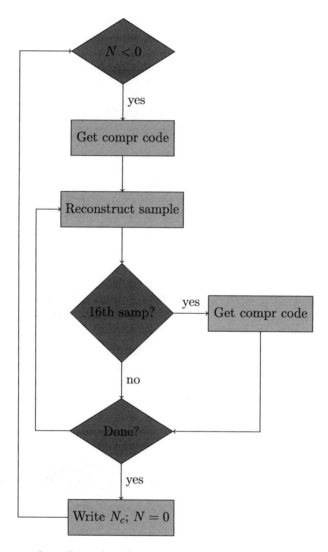

Figure 10-1. Flowchart for decompression of samples

Figure 10-2. *Riding the cog railway down. Mt. Washington Railway. By Benjamin West Kilburn (1827–1909). Reproduced from an original stereographic card published by Kilburn Brothers, Littleton, New Hampshire, Public Domain, https://commons.wikimedia.org/w/ index.php?curid=20253073.*

10.1 Getting the Sign Right

Remember, packBuf contains sample 0 (the low 3 bytes) and differences between the j-th and j-1 sample. The length of the difference is stored (as 2 bits at the appropriate location) in the long array comprCodeBuf.

To regenerate the samples, we need to first get the difference value and make it a proper long. Let's say the difference between two samples was equal to -200, which would be represented as a 2s-complement long:

11111111	11111111	11111111	0011 1000

Because the absolute value of the number is greater than 127, this will be stored in 2 bytes in packBuf, as shown here:

packBuf[0]:	0011 1000
packBuf[1]:	1111 1111

To reconstruct the original number, we have to *sign-extend* the high bit of the second byte. If that bit is 1 (as it is here), then we must put 1s in all the bits of the upper 2 bytes as well.

10.2 Overall Flowchart

Figure 10-1 shows the flowchart. We trigger the decompression by setting $N < 0$ (myns) to signal the PASM cog that we want decompression rather than compression (recall, for compression, we set $N > 0$).

The cog will read a compression code long and, based on the codes, read the correct number of bytes from packBuf. It will then reconstruct a sample. Every 16th sample, it will read a new compression code from hub memory. Finally, after processing all the samples, it will set $N = 0$.

Once the PASM cog completes the decompression, it will set myns to zero and set myncompr to the number of bytes read from packBuf during the decompression. (This can be used as a check on the decompression; it should be equal to ncompr from the compression stage.)

10.3 Spin Code

Listing 10-1 shows the Spin code for decompression.

Listing 10-1. Decompression Method in Spin That Triggers the PASM Decompression Cog

```
1    PUB DECOMPRESS(psampsBuf, ns, ppackBuf, ncompr, pcomprcodeBuf)
2    " Inputs : psampsBuf - address of long array of samples ↵
     (max len mymax)
3    "          ns - number of samples to decompress
4    "          ppackBuf - address of byte array of packed data
5    "          pcomprCodeBuf - address of long array of ↵
                compression codes
6    " Output : ncompr - number of bytes unpacked from packBuf
7    " Modified : sampsBuf
8      myns := 0
9      myncompr := 0
10
11     sampsBufAddr := psampsBuf
12     packBufAddr := ppackBuf
13     comprCodeBufAddr := pcomprCodeBuf
14
15     ' this will start the decompression
16     ' set to negative ns to trigger decompression
```

```
17    myns := -ns
18
19    ' when myns is zero, the decompression is complete
20    repeat until myns == 0
21    return myncompr
```

10.4 PASM: Main Decompression Loop

We will use the same cog as in the previous chapter but will trigger a decompression if myns < 0 (in the previous chapter, myns > 0 was a signal to start a compression). See Listing 10-2.

Listing 10-2. Decompression Code in PASM; Initialization

```
1     mov _ccodebitidx, #0
2     mov _ccodelongidx, #0
3
4  ' ADD THESE LINES >>>
5     ' check for compression or decompression ?
6     abs r0, _cns wc ' C set if nsamps < 0
7     if_c jmp #:decompress
8  ' ADD THESE LINES <<<
9
10    call #GET_SAMPLE
11    mov _cprev, _csamp ' save sample for diff
12    call #HANDLE_SAMP0
```

Here we add two lines in the initialization section: abs r0, _cns wc will take the absolute value of _cns and set C if _cns is negative. If so, jump to :decompress.

Listing 10-3 shows the decompression code.

Listing 10-3. Decompression Code in PASM; Details

```
1   : decompress ' _cns negative
2
3       rdlong _ccomprcode, _ccomprcodebufptr
4       mov _cncompr, #0
5       mov _cj, #0
6
7       call #MK_SAMP0
8       call #PUT_SAMPLE
9
10      add _cj, #1 'sample number j
11      add _cns, #1 wz
12      if_z jmp #:donedecomp
13
14  ' and the rest of the samps
15  : loopdecompns
16      call #MK_SAMPJ
17      call #PUT_SAMPLE
18      add _cj, #1
19      add _cns, #1
20
21      ' every 16th sample, read a new comprcode long
22      test _cj, #15 wz
23      if_nz jmp #:testns
24      add _ccomprcodebufptr, #4
25      rdlong _ccomprcode, _ccomprcodebufptr
26
27  : testns
28      tjnz _cns, #:loopdecompns
```

```
29
30  : donedecomp
31      wrlong _cncompr, _cncomprPtr
32      ' signal decompression complete
33      wrlong _cns, _cnsPtr
34      jmp #:mainLoop
```

You should recognize most of the code, explained here:

- **Lines 3–5**: Get the first compression code long and initialize the variables ncompr and j.

- **Lines 7–8**: Make sample 0 from packBuf and write it to sampsBuf in the hub (subroutines are explained in the next section).

- **Lines 10–12**: Here we *add* 1 to _cns because it starts out at -ns. When it is zero, we are done.

- **Lines 15–28**: Loop over the remaining samples.

- **Lines 22–25**: During this loop, every 16th sample, read a new compression code long from hub memory.

- **Lines 28–34**: Once we have processed all the samples, set myncompr to the number of bytes read from packBuf and set myns to zero to signal the completion of decompression.

10.5 Subroutines for Unpacking

Listings 10-4, 10-5 and 10-6 shows the three new subroutines.

Listing 10-4. Decompression Code in PASM; Subroutine to Save a Sample to the Hub After Reconstruction

```
1  PUT_SAMPLE
2  ' put a sample from _csamp to HUB sampsBuf
3    wrlong _csamp, _csampsbufPtr
4    add _csampsbufPtr, #4
5    PUT_SAMPLE_ret ret
```

PUT SAMPLE should be obvious: write the reconstructed sample back to hub memory and increment the pointer. See Listing 10-5.

Listing 10-5. Decompression Code in PASM; Subroutine to Reconstruct the First Sample

```
1  MK_SAMP0 ' decompress samp 0
2  ' read from HUB packbuf to _csamp for samp0 (3 bytes)
3      mov r0, #0
4      mov _csamp, #0
5  :read3
6      rdbyte r1, _cpackbufPtr
7      shl r1, r0
8      or _csamp, r1
9      add _cpackbufPtr, #1
10     add r0, #8
11     cmp r0, #24 wz
12     if_nz jmp #:read3
13
14     rol _csamp, #8 ' sign extend
15     sar _csamp, #8
```

```
16
17        ' update ncompr and code
18        add _cncompr, #3
19        shr _ccomprcode, #2 ' remove samp0 code ...
20        MK_SAMP0_ret ret
```

MK_SAMP0 reads 3 bytes from packBuf and places them in the correct spots in _csamp.

- **Lines 3–4**: r0 is the number of bits to shift each byte of packBuf. r1 is the current byte read from packBuf and shifted by 0, then 8, then 16 bits (bytes 0, 1, and 2, respectively).

- **Lines 5–12**: Loop three times to :read3 (r0 = 0, 8, and 16). When r0==24, break out of the loop. The sign bit for the sample isn't correctly set yet (the upper byte, which is byte 3, containing bits 31–24 are all zero. However, if the sample was originally negative, those bits should all be 1. Luckily, that information (about whether the sample was originally negative or positive) is in the most significant bit of byte 2 (bit 23). If the sample was originally negative before compression, bits 23 would have been 1; if the sample was positive, bit 23 would be 0. The instruction rol _csamp, #8 shifts bits 23–0 up to bits 31–8, and sar _csamp, #8 then shifts the bits back to the right *but preserves the sign of the long.* In other words, we shift bit 23 to bit 31 (rol) and then shift bit 31 back to 23, but if it is a 1, then bits 31–23 are set to 1. If that MSB is a zero, then those bits are set to 0.

- **Lines 18–19**: Update ncompr and comprCode.

Finally, Listing 10-6 shows the reconstruction of the j-th sample by properly making the difference and adding it to the previous sample.

Listing 10-6. Decompression Code in PASM; Subroutine to Reconstruct a Sample

```
1   MK_SAMPJ
2       mov r0, #0 ' number of bytes
3       mov _cdiff, #0
4       mov r1, _ccomprcode
5       and r1, #3 ' get compr code for this samp. (2 low bits)
6       shr _ccomprcode, #2 ' and prep for next loop ...
7
8       ' byte 0 - right most
9       rdbyte r2, _cpackbufPtr
10      add _cpackbufPtr, #1
11      mov _cdiff, r2
12      add r0, #1
13      cmp r1, _ccode08 wz ' check r1 (code)
14
15      if_z jmp #:shiftde
16
17      ' byte 1
18      rdbyte r2, _cpackbufPtr
19      add _cpackbufPtr, #1
20      rol r2, #8
21      or _cdiff, r2
22      add r0, #1
23
24      cmp r1, _ccode16 wz
25      if_z jmp #:shiftde
26
```

```
27        ' byte 2
28        rdbyte r2, _cpackbufPtr
29        add _cpackbufPtr, #1
30        rol r2, #16
31        or _cdiff, r2
32        add r0, #1
33
34  : shiftde
35        ' set the sign of the diff correctly by sign extending ...
36        ' 1 byte diff ...
37        cmp r0, #1 wz
38        if_nz jmp #:sh2
39        rol _cdiff, #24 ' sign extend
40        sar _cdiff, #24
41        jmp #:donede
42
43        ' 2 byte diff ...
44  :sh2
45        cmp r0, #2 wz
46        if_nz jmp #:sh3
47        rol _cdiff, #16 ' sign extend
48        sar _cdiff, #16
49        jmp #:donede
50
51        ' 3 byte diff ...
52  :sh3
53        rol _cdiff, #8 ' sign extend
54        sar _cdiff, #8
55
56  : donede
```

```
57        ' add sample to prev
58        add _csamp, _cdiff
59        ' now mask off the high byte and sign extend the 3 lower
60        rol _csamp, #8
61        sar _csamp, #8
62        add _cncompr, r0 ' update ncompr
63   MK_SAMPJ_ret ret
```

MK SAMPJ tests the value of the compression code for the j-th sample and reads 1, 2, or 3 bytes from packBuf accordingly. It writes those bytes to _cdiff (with the dance of shifting left and right to get the sign right) and then adds _cdiff to _csamp to get the current sample (again, with the shift left/right dance).

- **Lines 2–6**: Initialize variables. r0 is number of bytes to read, r1 is the compression code, and r2 will be the byte read from packBuf.

- **Lines 9–15**: Read a byte, place it in _cdiff, and check the code to see whether we are done.

- **Lines 13–25**: If code was CODE08, then we're done. If not, then get another byte, shift it left by 8, and or it with _cdiff.

- **Lines 28–32**: Again, these lines will properly set byte 2 if necessary (if the compression code is CODE16).

- **Lines 34–54**: If only 1 byte was read (r0==1), then shift _cdiff by 24 bits up and then back down. If 2 bytes were read, then shift by 16; if 3 were read, then shift by 8; and so on.

- **Lines 58–62**: Add _cdiff to _csamp (the previous sample), shift it up by 8, and then shift it back down and return.

10.6 Testing Decompression of Two Samples

The testing is straightforward: compress the samples and then decompress them. In between the compression and decompression, I set sampsBuf to zero, so I know that the values in sampsBuf after decompression were in fact generated by the decompression code. Compare these values for sampsBuf with the original numbers.

```
1    PUB MAIN
2    ...
3      TEST_THAT_SAMP0_IS_PROPERLY_UNPACKED
4      TEST_THAT_SAMP1_IS_PROPERLY_UNPACKED
5    ...
6    PRI TEST_THAT_SAMP0_IS_PROPERLY_UNPACKED | t0, nc, nc1, ns, d
7      nsamps := 1
8      d := $FF_FF_AB_CD
9      sampsBuf[0] := d
10     nc := COMPR.COMPRESS (@sampsBuf, nsamps, @packBuf, ↵
       @comprCodeBuf)
11     sampsBuf[0] := 0
12
13     nc1 := COMPR.DECOMPRESS (@sampsBuf, nsamps, @packBuf, ↵
       nc, @comprCodeBuf)
14
15     t0 := (nc == nc1) & (sampsBuf[0] == d)
16     TDD.ASSERT_TRUTHY (t0, string (" Test that sample 0 is ↵
       properly unpacked from packBuf "))
17
18     PRI TEST_THAT_SAMP1_IS_PROPERLY_UNPACKED | t0, nc, nc1, ↵
       ns, s0, s1
```

```
19      nsamps := 2
20      s0 := $FF_FA_09_19
21      s1 := $FF_FA_4F_2E
22      sampsBuf[0] := s0
23      sampsBuf[1] := s1
24      nc := COMPR.COMPRESS (@sampsBuf, nsamps, @packBuf, ↵
        @comprCodeBuf)
25      sampsBuf[0] := 0
26      sampsBuf[1] := 0
27
28      nc1 := COMPR.DECOMPRESS (@sampsBuf, nsamps, @packBuf, nc, ↵
        @comprCodeBuf)
29      t0 := (nc == nc1) & (sampsBuf[1] == s1)
30      TDD.ASSERT_TRUTHY (t0, string(" Test that sample 1 is ↵
        properly unpacked from packBuf "))
```

The test should pass, as shown here:

```
Test that sample 0 is properly unpacked from packBuf
...ok
Test that sample 1 is properly unpacked from packBuf
...ok
```

10.7 Testing Decompression of 128 Samples

OK, that worked. Let's try it with 128 samples. We will generate 128 pseudorandom numbers. Listing 10-7 shows the Spin instructions.

Listing 10-7. Testing the Decompression Code; 128 Samples Initialized

```
1    j := 0
2    sampsBuf[j] := cnt ' seed it with counter
3    ?sampsBuf[j] ' pseudorandom number
4    sampsBuf[j] &= $FF_FF_FF ' low 3 bytes only
5
6    sampsBuf[j] <<= 8 ' sign extend
7    sampsBuf[j] ~>= 8
8    sav[j] := sampsBuf[j]
```

These instructions will seed the sample with the current value of the counter and then use that seed to look up a pseudorandom number. The number has to be limited to 3 bytes, so we mask off those 3 bytes and then sign-extend the upper bit.

The compression, decompression, and testing are done as shown in Listing 10-8.

Listing 10-8. Testing the Decompression Code; Stub Showing Test Results

```
1    nc := COMPR.COMPRESS (@sampsBuf, nsamps, @packBuf, ↵
     @comprCodeBuf)
2
3    repeat j from 0 to nsamps -1
4      sampsBuf[j] := 0
```

```
5
6      nc1 := COMPR.DECOMPRESS (@sampsBuf, nsamps, @packBuf, nc, ↵
       @comprCodeBuf)

7
8      t0 := (nc == nc1)
9      repeat j from 0 to nsamps -1
10         t1 := (sampsBuf[j] == sav[j])
11         t0 &= t1
```

The samples are compressed, the sampsBuf array is cleared, and the samples are decompressed. We then check that the number of compressed and decompressed bytes is equal (nc==nc1) and that the samples are equal to their saved values.

```
1    PUB MAIN
2    ...
3      TEST_THAT_128_SAMPS_PROPERLY_COMPRESS_AND_DECOMPRESS
4    ...
5    PRI TEST_THAT_128_SAMPS_PROPERLY_COMPRESS_AND_DECOMPRESS | ↵
     t0, t1, j, nc, nc1, sav [128]
6      nsamps := 128

7
8      j := 0
9      sampsBuf[j] := cnt ' seed it with counter
10     ?sampsBuf[j] ' pseudorandom number
11     sampsBuf[j] &= $FF_FF_FF ' low 3 bytes only

12
13     sampsBuf[j] <<= 8 ' sign extend
14     sampsBuf[j] ~>= 8
15     sav[j] := sampsBuf[j]

16
17     repeat j from 1 to nsamps -1
```

```
18            sampsBuf[j] := sampsBuf[j -1]
19            ?sampsBuf[j] ' pseudorandom numbers
20            sampsBuf[j] &= $FF_FF_FF ' low 3 bytes only
21            sampsBuf[j] <<= 8 ' sign extend
22            sampsBuf[j] ~>= 8
23            sav[j] := sampsBuf[j]
24
25     nc := COMPR.COMPRESS (@sampsBuf, nsamps, @packBuf, ↵
       @comprCodeBuf)
26
27     repeat j from 0 to nsamps -1
28       sampsBuf[j] := 0
29
30     nc1 := COMPR.DECOMPRESS (@sampsBuf, nsamps, @packBuf, nc,↵
         @comprCodeBuf)
31
32     t0 := (nc == nc1)
33     repeat j from 0 to nsamps -1
34         t1 := (sampsBuf[j] == sav[j])
35         t0 &= t1
36
37     TDD.ASSERT_TRUTHY (t0, string(" Test that compression ↵
       and decompression of 128 random numbers is successful "))
```

Next run the test, as shown here:

```
Test that compression and decompression of 128 random numbers
is successful
***FAIL
```

Oh no! What went wrong? Let's do some debugging in the next chapter. As you can see in Figure 10-3, there are real-world consequences to engineering or user mistakes!

Figure 10-3. *Derailment at Eastwood Junction, 1948.* https://
upload.wikimedia.org/wikipedia/commons/4/4a/Derailment_at_
Eastwood%2C_1948_%285247093755%29.jpg.

CHAPTER 11

Debugging PASM Code

It is relatively straightforward to debug Spin code. You can insert commands to print the value of variables to the terminal. This is a time-honored way to debug code, and though tedious, it works. In Listings 11-1 and 11-2, I show how I monitor the value of a variable.

Listing 11-1. Debugging Spin Code with Print Commands

```
1   PUB MAIN
2   ...
3     UARTS.STR(DEBUG, string(" nsamps = "))
4     UARTS.DEC(DEBUG, nsamps)
5     UARTS.PUTC(DEBUG, CR)
```

Insert print statements like this in your Spin code, and you can examine the value of variables at different places.

I find that the verbose set of commands gets inconvenient, so I have defined a method called PRINTF.

© Sridhar Anandakrishnan 2018
S. Anandakrishnan, *Propeller Programming*, https://doi.org/10.1007/978-1-4842-3354-2_11

Listing 11-2. Convenience Method to Print Out a Variable's Value

```
1
2   PUB MAIN
3   ...
4     PRINTF(DEBUG, string(" nc "), nc, 1)
5   ...
6   '
7   ' Convenience method to print `n' to port `p' with the ↵
    following format :
8   ' PRINTF(DEBUG, string(" nc "), nc, 1)
9   ' nc :3, 0x03, 0 b0000011
10  PRI PRINTF(p, lbl, n, len)
11  ' p is the serial port, lbl is the string label
12  ' n is the number to print
13  ' len is the number of bytes to display in the hex and binary
14     UARTS.STR(p, lbl)
15     UARTS.PUTC(p, COLON)
16     UARTS.DEC(p, n)
17     UARTS.STR(p, string(COMMA, " 0x"))
18     UARTS.HEX(p, n, len *2)
19     UARTS.STR(p, string(COMMA, " 0b"))
20     UARTS.BIN(p, n, len *8)
21     UARTS.PUTC(p, CR)
22     UARTS.PUTC(p, LF)
```

We can't do the same in PASM code, though. There isn't a simple way to print to the terminal from PASM code, so I will demonstrate two different methods for examining variable values in PASM. These methods of debugging are referred to as logging (see Figure 11-1 for another example of logging; the size of those logs is astonishing and the sight of them cut down is quite sad!)

Figure 11-1. *Redwood logs on train from forest to mill.* https://
upload.wikimedia.org/wikipedia/commons/9/9a/Redwood_
Logging_Train.jpg.

11.1 Logging to a Hub Array

The first logging technique is to save values to a hub array that can be
printed out at leisure. The second is to write a long from one cog to another
(from a PASM cog to a Spin cog) using a set of hardware pins and Serial
Peripheral Interface (SPI). Here I will look at the first technique.
We already looked at the SPI logging in Chapter 7.

1. We will define a new array in Spin called logBuf.

2. We will define a new variable in the PASM code
    called clogBufPtr.

3. Before the cog is launched, we will place the address
    of logBuf into clogBufPtr.

Recall from Chapter 6 that there are two ways to pass parameters to a
PASM cog: by using the cognew command and by storing the parameter in the
cog code before it is launched. We are using the second method in Listing 11-3.

215

Listing 11-3. Debugging PASM Code by Passing the Address of the
Log Buffer in a Register

```
1   CON
2     LOGLEN = 256
3
4   VAR
5     logBuf[LOGLEN]
6
7   PUB START
8     _clogBufPtr := @logBuf
9     ccogid := cognew(@STEIM, @myns)
10  ...
11
12  DAT 'pasm cog
13  STEIM ORG 0
14
15  ... instructions
16    rdlong _cns _cnsPtr wz
17
18  ... variables
19  _ccode24 long CODE24
20
21  _clogBufPtr long 0
22
23  ... reserved space
24  _cnsPtr res 1
25
26  FIT 496
27  ... system registers (PAR, CNT, etc)
```

We can now write to logBuf from PASM, and the Spin code can print out those values. There is one important caveat: the PASM code and the Spin code run at very different speeds. The PASM code will populate the logBuf array, and at some later time, the Spin code will print it out. For that reason, you should include a label during logging. This label will be some unique identifier that tells you where the log value was written, during which iteration of the loop, and so on.

11.2 Spin Code

Add the following to steim_pasm.spin:

```
1   CON
2     LOGLEN = 256
3   ...
4   VAR
5     byte logIdx
6
7     long logBuf[LOGLEN]
8
9   PUB GETLOG
10  '' return address of log array
11    return @logBuf
12
13  PUB GETLOGLEN
14  '' return length of log
15    return logIdx
```

Here we define a new array where the log values will be stored, as well as new methods GETLOG and GETLOGLEN that return the address and populated length of that array.

In the main Spin file `steim_pasm_Demo.spin`, you can use the code in Listing 11-4 to print out the contents of the log array.

Listing 11-4. Debugging PASM Code by Sharing a Log Buffer; Spin Code

```
 1  VAR
 2    byte loglen
 3    long logBufPtr
 4
 5  PUB MAIN
 6  ...
 7
 8  logBufPtr := COMPR.GETLOG
 9  loglen := COMPR.GETLOGLEN
10  repeat j from 0 to loglen -1
11    UARTS.HEX(DEBUG, long [logBufPtr][j], 8)
```

11.3 PASM Code

Populating the log array is done with `wrlong` instructions in PASM. The hub address of the log array is available in `_clogBufPtr`. We first save that value to `_clogBufPtrSav` so that we can reset to that location when we reach the end of the array.

In Listing 11-5, we implement the logging code. In addition to the storage for the logged data itself, we define a variable `_clogIdx` and a constant `_clogMaxIdx`. Every time we write to the log array, we increment the former; when the index reaches the end of the array, we reset the index to the beginning of the array.

Listing 11-5. Debugging PASM Code by Sharing a Log Buffer; PASM
Code

```
1
2   mov r0, par
3   add r0, #16
4   rdlong _ccomprcodebufPtr, r0
5
6   ''>>> ADD THIS TO INITIALIZATION SECTION OF PASM CODE
7     call #INIT_LOG
8   ''<<<
9     mov _cj, #0 ' j-th samp
10
11  ''>>> ADD THESE SUBROUTINE DEFENITIONS
12  INIT_LOG
13    mov _clogIdx, #0
14    mov _clogBufPtr, _clogBufPtrSav
15  INIT_LOG_ret ret
16
17  LOG
18  '' write logVal to logBuf
19  '' increment logIdx
20  '' treat as circular buffer
21    wrlong _clogVal, _clogBufPtr
22    add _clogBufPtr, #4
23    add _clogIdx, #1
24    wrlong _clogIdx, _clogIdxPtr
25
26    ' wrap around ?
```

```
27    test _clogIdx, _clogMaxIdx wz
28    if_nz jmp #:logdone
29
30    mov _clogIdx, #0
31    mov _clogBufPtr, _clogBufPtrSav
32  :logdone
33  LOG_ret ret
34
35  ...
36
37  ''>>> ADD THESE VARIABLE DECLARATIONS
38  _clogMaxIdx long LOGLEN -1 ' 0 to loglen -1
39  _clogIdx long 0
40  _clogVal long 0
41
42  _clogBufPtr long 0
43  _clogBufPtrSav long 0
44  ...
```

The LOG subroutine keeps track of the index into the log array and resets to the start when it reaches the end. It writes the value in _clogVal to the current address in the log array, increments that address, and resets the address to the beginning of the array if needed.

11.4 Bug Fix

The failure at the end of the previous chapter can now be tracked down. By placing the following statements at strategic places, I discovered that I had made a mistake in writing the compression code longs:

```
mov _clogVal, xxx
call #LOG
```

When there are 128 samples, the compression code array is 8 longs in length (2 bits per sample). However, I was mistakenly writing *a ninth* long, which overwrote memory of another array. (As it turns out, this was the packBuf array, but it could have been anything.)

Figure 11-2 shows the compression flowchart again, but I have added a check to the right of "16th samp?" shape. If this is also the last sample, jump out of the loop and finalize.

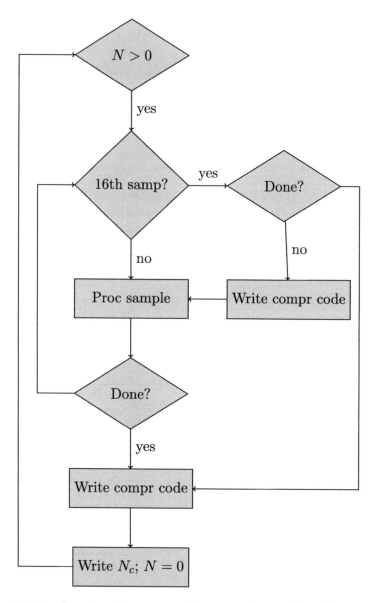

Figure 11-2. *Flowchart for processing samples, with addition of a check for the final sample before writing the compression code. Compare this figure to Figure 9-1.*

If, for example, there are exactly 16 samples to compress, the compression code is *written only once*.

On the first sample to the 15th sample, control flows down from "16th samp?" to "Done?" and then back up to "16th samp?"

On the last sample, the "16th samp?" query is true, so we go to the right, but the "Done?" query is also true, so we exit the loop and write the compression code at the end (without that question, we would write the compression code twice). In Figure 11-3, we show the consequences of over-running ones bounds!

Figure 11-3. *Train wreck at Gare Montparnasse, Paris, 1895. The train entered the station at a dangerously fast 40-60km/hr, and when the air brake on the locomotive failed, the train crossed the entire concourse (100m) and crashed through a 60cm thick wall before falling to the street below.*

PASM code will allow you modify *any* memory location. There is no checking of array lengths or bounds. It's all up to you!

PART III

C Language

CHAPTER 12

C Programming
for the Propeller

Parallax and the community have put enormous effort into bringing a C compiler to the Propeller. The advantage to using C is that it is a stable, established language with a large knowledge base. In addition, there are hundreds of books and web sites devoted to teaching C, and you can use many libraries and pieces of example code in your programs. Many of the programs that run the backbone (or the engine, Figure 12-1) of the Internet are written in C.

© Sridhar Anandakrishnan 2018
S. Anandakrishnan, *Propeller Programming*, https://doi.org/10.1007/978-1-4842-3354-2_12

Figure 12-1. *In the engineer's cab on the Chicago and Northwestern Railroad. Photographer Jack Delano, Library of Congress, Farm Security Administration archives (https://goo.gl/pHmY5t).*

12.1 The C Language

This section is a short primer on C. I encourage you to get a copy of *The C Programming Language* by Brian Kernighan and Dennis Ritchie, which is the authoritative guide to C. Here are a few important rules to remember:

- C is case sensitive.

- Statements must end with a semicolon (;).

- Blocks are enclosed in paired curly braces (indentation is not important).

```
1  while (x < 100) {
2    x += 1;
3  }
```

- Block comments have /* at the beginning and */ at the end. Line comments start with //.

- Variable naming follows the same rules as in Spin.

- Numbers are in decimal if naked, hexadecimal if preceded by 0x, and binary if preceded by b.

```
1  /* a block comment
2   * three assignments that do the same thing
3   */
4  x = 42; // decimal . This is a line comment
5  x = 0x2A; // hex
6  x = b00101010; // binary
```

Here are some Spin and C parallels:

- **CON**: The equivalent of the CON block in Spin is the #define statement, as shown in Listing 12-1.

Listing 12-1. define Statements in C

```
1  #define NSAMPS_MAX 128
```

OBJ: The equivalent of the OBJ block in Spin is the #include statement, as shown in Listing 12-2.

Listing 12-2. #include Statements in C

```
1  #include <stdio.h>
2  #include <propeller.h>
```

VAR: Variables can be defined as either *local* variables that are available only within a function or as *global* variables that are available to all functions in the program. To define (reserve space for) a variable, do the following:

```
1  int nsamps, ncompr;
2  char packBuf[512];
3  unsigned int spiSem;
```

Variable definitions are either for individuals (nsamps, etc.) or for arrays (packBuf[512]). The type of the variable precedes its name. Variables types are the integers char, short, int (8-, 16-, and 32-bit, respectively), and a 32-bit float. The integer types can be either signed or unsigned.

Assignment and math: These are similar to Spin but use an equal sign instead of :=. Addition, multiplication, and division are the same as in Spin. The modulo operator is the percent sign (%).

```
1  int x, y, z;
2  x = 12;
3  x += 42;
4  y = x/5;    // integer division
5  z = x % 5; // remainder of x/5
6  z = x++;    // post - increment: increment x, and store in z
7  z = ++x;    // pre - increment: store x in z, then increment x
```

Relational and logical operators: These are similar to Spin, but with these differences:

- The *not equal* operator is !=.

- The AND operator is && and the OR operator is ||.

- The NOT operator is !.

- The "*less-than-or-equal* and "*greater-than-or-equal*" relations are <= and >=."

In conditional statements, 0 (zero) is false, and any nonzero value is true.

Flow control: There are four flow control statements.

- This is a for loop:

```
1   /* for (<init >; <end condition >; <per - loop action >)
2    * The most common for - loop runs N times
3    * number of times as below.
4    * An infinite loop is for (;;) { <stmts > }.
5    * (you can have blank init, end or per - loop)
6    */
7   for(i=0; i<N; i++) {
8       x++;
9       y--;
10  }
```

- These are while and do...while:

```
1   // while loop. The block only runs if the relation is true.
2   while (x < 100) {
3       y++;
4   }
5   // do ... while loop. The block always runs once
6   // and then check the relation.
```

```
7  do {
8    y++
9  } while (x < 100);
```

- This is a switch...case:

```
1  switch(menuItems) {
2  case MENUITEM0:      // if menuItems == MENUITEM0,
3    do_menu0();         // execute block up to the break.
4    break;
5    /*** DANGER **
6     * you must have a break at the end
7     * of the case block.
8     * the break will return control to the switch.
9     * without the break, control will pass to the
10    * next case block.
11    *** YOU WERE WARNED **
12    */
13  case MENUITEM1:
14    do_menu1();
15    break;
16  default: // you can include a case that handles
17           // unknown values
18    handle_unknownMenu();
19  }
```

Pointers and arrays: Every variable and array has a memory address. The address of variables is given thusly:

```
1  int x;
2  /* this defines a pointer to an int */
3  int *px;
```

```
4   x = 42;

5

6   /* this obtains the address of x and stores it in px */

7   px = &x;

8

9   /* this obtains the value stored at the location

10      pointed to by px */

11  y = *px; // now y is 42
```

Arrays are stored in contiguous memory, and the address of the array is the address of the first element of the array.

```
1   int sampsBuf[128];

2   int packBuf[512];

3

4   // arrays are zero -based, sampsBuf[0]... sampsBuf[127]

5   y = sampsBuf[12];

6

7   // the memory address of an array is obtained by

8   // referring to the array.

9   // the n-th element of the array is obtained by

10  // adding n to the address, treating that as a pointer

11  // here we get the 12 th element (12 th int) of sampsBuf

12  y = *(sampsBuf +12);

13

14  // the compiler knows that packbuf is a char array

15  // so packBuf +12 refers to the 12 th element (12 th byte),

16  // in this case

17  z = *(packBuf +12);
```

Pointer arithmetic is needed when you want to modify the value of variables in a function.

```
1   ...
2   int main() {
3     int x = 42;
4     int y;
5     int *px = &x;
6     y = incrementNum(x);
7     // x is still 42, but y is 43.
8     incrementNumPtr (px);
9     // x is now 43.
10  }
11
12  /* incrementNum - increment a variable
13   * args: n - variable to be incremented
14   * return: incremented value
15   */
16  int incrementNum(int n) { // n is a local copy of x. x is ⏎
    unaffected.
17    return (n++);
18  }
19
20  /* incrementNumPtr - increment the value of a variable.
21   * args: *pn - a pointer to an int
22   * return: none
23   * effect: the variable pointed to by pn is incremented
24   */
25  void incrementNumPtr(int *pn) {
26    // pn is a pointer to the int, and *pn is the int itself
27    *pn++; // * binds tightly, so parens (* pn)++ not needed.
28  }
```

12.2 Programming the Propeller in C

To program the Propeller with C code, we have to recognize a few constraints of the device. The first, and most critical, is that hub memory is limited to 32KB and that cog RAM is limited to 2KB. Next, the Propeller has eight cogs, and the C compiler and linker have to handle launching new cogs properly. In this book, I will discuss three cases (cases that I think cover most of the likely projects).

SimpleIDE creates a *workspace* when you first install it. If you have downloaded the repository from `https://github.com/sanandak/propbook-code.git`, then there is a SimpleIDE workspace in `propbook-code`. Select Tools ➤ Properties and set the workspace to the downloaded directory (`.../propbook-code/SimpleIDE`).

- If the size of the C program (after compiling) is less than approximately 30KB, then it will fit entirely in hub memory. The compiler will place your code into hub along with a *kernel* (approximately sized 2KB, for a total size of less than 32KB). The kernel is a program that copies instructions from your code into a cog and executes them. This is known as the *large memory model* (LMM). The main drawback of LMM is that every instruction resides in the hub and is copied to cog memory before execution, slowing down the program. In almost every way, though, this is a standard C program. Cogs can be launched and stopped; the counters and special registers like `ina` and `outa` can be read and set; the locks can be used; and so on.

- If there is a need for a faster speed from some part of the program, we can place that C code in a Cog-C file (with the extension .cogc). This part of the code must compile to assembly code that is less than 2KB in size, and it will be placed into cog RAM and run at full speed. The rest of the program will continue to operate under LMM mode. I call this the *mixed-mode Cog-C model*. The advantage is that the program will run at full speed. The drawback is that the assembly code produced by the compiler may not be as efficient as code that you write.

- The final model is where the speed-critical code is written in PASM and is saved on a cog. This cog is now fully under your control. You can optimize it for your needs (of course, as with the previous case, the code has to be less than 2KB in size). The rest of the code continues to run under LMM. This is called the *mixed-mode PASM model*.

12.2.1 SimpleIDE

To write the code, compile and link it, download it to the Propeller, and view the output, we will use the SimpleIDE application, which is an integrated development environment (IDE). This is a cross-platform IDE (Windows, Linux, and macOS) that is aware of all three of the models and does the detailed work of compiling the programs correctly and linking them in the right way.

The place to start with SimpleIDE is at http://learn.propeller.com where you can download the program and step through a series of excellent tutorials on using the program and developing LMM projects (see Figure 12-2).

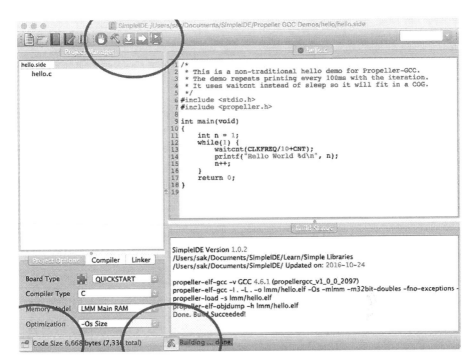

Figure 12-2. *SimpleIDE window with Project Manager button, Build Window button (at bottom of picture), and Build button (the hammer at the top of the picture) highlighted*

There are three tabs in the Project Manager: the Project Options tab, the Compiler tab, and the Linker tab. The settings shown in Figure 12-3 are good for the examples in this book, so make sure you set yours properly.

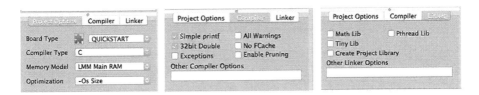

Figure 12-3. *Settings for the Project Options, Compiler, and Linker tabs*

12.2.2 Hello World

After installing SimpleIDE, you will have a number of examples in the
Propeller GCC Demos folder (in the SimpleIDE workspace). One of those
is called Welcome. Open the project file Welcome.side and build it; you
should see messages in the build window ending with "Build Succeeded!"
At the bottom of the window a message shows the size of the program
(in this case, about 7KB). If the program successfully builds, you can
download and run it on the Propeller and have the output displayed on a
terminal by clicking the icon at the top that shows a screen with an arrow.

I have modified the code slightly, but it is very straightforward, as
shown in Listing 12-3.

Listing 12-3. Hello World Program in C (SimpleIDE/My Projects/
ch11/Welcome.c)

```
1  # include <stdio.h>
2  # include <propeller.h>
3
4  int main(void) {
5      int n = 1;
6      while (1) {
7          waitcnt(CLKFREQ/10 + CNT);
8          printf(" Hello World %d\n", n);
9          n++;
10      }
11      return 0;
12  }
```

Lines 1–2: The stdio library has the printf function. However,
because it is a complex (and large) function, the Compiler tab includes
the option to use a "Simple printf" that reduces the size somewhat. The
propeller library has the Propeller-specific functions such as waitcnt and
waitpeq and the special registers such as CNT, INA, and so on.

Lines 4–13: The main program is similar to the PUB MAIN method in Spin. This function shouldn't exit; it should initialize some variables and then enter an infinite loop.

Line 5: Define the variable n and initialize it to 1.

Line 6: Enter an infinite loop.

Line 7: waitcnt is similar to the waitcnt in Spin, but it has only one argument. The processor will pause at this line until the counter value is equal to the argument of waitcnt. In this case, this is the current count value plus 1 second. The variable CLKFREQ contains the number of counts in 1 second (generally 80 million at top speed, but it depends on the external crystal and the phase-locked loop value).

Line 8: The printf function prints a formatted string to the terminal. Look at the manual page for printf for how to format numbers. In short, %d prints a decimal number, %x prints the number in hexadecimal format, and %f prints a floating-point value.

Line 9: Increment the value of n.

Running the program will result in the following in the terminal window with a new message every tenth of a second:

```
Hello World 1
Hello World 2
Hello World 3
...
```

12.2.3 Launching a New Cog

To launch a new cog in LMM, we must define a function and then pass that function to the cogstart function.

Start a new C project (Open ➤ New) named compr_cog0. Set the Project Options, Compiler, and Linker options as before.

For the purposes of display and discussion, I have split the file compr_ cog0.c into three separate parts, but really all three parts are in one file. Every multicog program will have these three parts.

Part 1 in Listing 12-4 is the front matter where the libraries are included, the shared memory for the *stack* and the shared variables is set aside, and the constants are defined.

Listing 12-4. Part 1: Front Matter for File compr_cog0.c

```
 1  /*
 2     compr - cog0.c - start a new cog to perform compression.
 3  */
 4
 5  /* libraries */
 6  # include <stdio.h>
 7  # include <propeller.h>
 8
 9  /* defines */
10
11  // size of stack in bytes
12  # define STACK_SIZE_BYTES 200
13  // compression constants
14  # define NSAMPS_MAX 128
15  # define CODE08 0b01
16  # define CODE16 0b10
17  # define CODE24 0b11
18  # define TWO_BYTES 0x7F // any diff values greater than ↩
    this are 2 bytes
19  # define THREE_BYTES 0 x7FF // diff values greater than ↩
    this are 3 bytes
20
21
```

```
22  /* global variables */
23  // reserved space to be passed to cogstart
24  static unsigned int comprCogStack[STACK_SIZE_BYTES >> 2];
25
26  // shared vars
27  volatile int nsamps;
28  volatile int ncompr;
29  volatile int sampsBuf[NSAMPS_MAX];
30  volatile char packBuf[NSAMPS_MAX <<2];  // 128 * 4
31  volatile int comprCodesBuf[NSAMPS_MAX >>4];  // 128 / 16
```

Line 12: The stack is a region of memory used by the kernel to store internal variables and state. It should be at least 150 bytes plus 4 bytes per function call in the cog.

Lines 14–19: Constants used by all cogs.

Line 24: Declare and reserve space for the stack here.

Lines 27–31: Shared variables have a volatile qualifier to signal the compiler not to remove them during optimization. If the compiler thinks a variable is unused, it won't reserve space for it. However, it is possible that a variable is used by a Spin or PASM cog unknown to the compiler.

Part 2, shown in Listing 12-5, is the code for the cog. Define a function that is called by the main cog. This function (and any functions that it calls) will run in a separate cog from the main cog. However, this cog will have access to the variables declared earlier. Those are global variables and available to all functions in the file.

Listing 12-5. Part 2: Compression Cog Code in File compr_cog0.c

```
1  /* cog code - comprCog
2      use nsamps and ncompr to signal with main cog
3          start compression when nsamps != 0
4          signal completion with ncompr > 0
```

```
 5        signal error with ncompr = 0
 6      compress sampsBuf to packBuf - NOT DONE YET
 7      populate comprCodesBuf - NOT DONE YET
 8      - args: pointer to memory space PAR - UNUSED
 9      - return: none
10    */
11  void comprCog(void *p) {
12    int i, nc, nbytes, codenum, codeshift, code;
13    int diff, adiff;
14
15    while (1) {
16      if (nsamps == 0) {
17        continue; // loop continuously while nsamps is 0
18      } else {
19        // perform the compression here
20        if (nsamps > NSAMPS_MAX || nsamps < -NSAMPS_MAX) {
21          ncompr = 0; // signal error
22          nsamps = 0;
23          continue;
24        }
25        ncompr = 3; // signal completion
26        nsamps = 0; // prevent another cycle from starting
27      }
28    }
29  }
```

Line 11: The cog function definition. void comprCog() means that this doesn't return any value. The argument (void *p) means that an address is passed in—this is the equivalent of PAR. However, because we are using the global variables to pass information between cogs, we won't use PAR.

Lines 12–13: Local variables used by the cog.

Line 15: Infinite loop that contains the actual code that does the work of the cog.

Lines 16–18: If nsamps is set to nonzero by main, enter the section that does the work.

Lines 20–26: Error checking and, finally, the work of this cog. Set ncompr to 3 and nsamps to 0. (We will add code to do the actual compression later.)

Part 3, shown in Listing 12-6, is the entry point for the program, including the main function and the code that runs first. Again, this cog has access to the global variables. It also starts the new cog and interacts with it by setting and reading variables in those global variables.

Listing 12-6. Part 3: Main Code in File compr_cog0.c

```
1   /* main cog - initializes variables and starts new cogs.
2    * don 't exit - start infinite loop as the last thing.
3    */
4   int main(void)
5   {
6     int comprCogId = -1;
7     int i;
8
9     nsamps = 0;
10    ncompr = -1;
11
12    printf(" starting main \n");
13
14    /* start a new cog with
15     * (1) address of function to run in the new cog
16     * (2) address of the memory to pass to the function
17     * (3) address of the stack
18     * (4) size of the stack, in bytes
19     */
```

```
20    comprCogId = cogstart (&comprCog, NULL, comprCogStack, ↵
      STACK_SIZE_BYTES);
21    if(comprCogId < 0) {
22      printf(" error starting compr cog \n");
23      while (1) {;}
24    }
25
26    printf(" started compression cog %d\n", comprCogId);
27
28    /* start the compression cog by setting nsamps to 1 */
29    sampsBuf[0] = 0xEFCDAB;
30    nsamps = 1;
31
32    /* wait until the compression cog sets ncompr to a non -neg, ↵
      number */
33    while(ncompr < 0) {
34      ;
35    }
36
37    printf(" nsamps = %d, ncompr = %d\n", nsamps, ncompr);
38    printf(" samp0 = %x, packBuf = %x %x %x\n", sampsBuf[0], ↵
      packBuf[0], packBuf[1], packBuf[2]);
39
40    while (1)
41    {
42      ;
43    }
44  }
```

Line 20: This is the key in main. The cogstart function takes four arguments. The first is the address of the function to place in the new cog: &comprCog. The ampersand symbol (&) in C is to obtain the address of a

244

variable or function. The next argument is the address of memory that will be passed to the cog in PAR (the "locker number" in the analogy in Chapter 6). In this case, because we are using global variables to exchange information, we won't use PAR and can pass NULL (which is, as it states, the null pointer). The third and fourth arguments are the address of the reserved stack space and its length in bytes, respectively. The stack is a region of memory that the kernel needs to store variables and counters.

Line 30: Here we set nsamps=1, which signals the compression cog to begin its work.

Lines 33–35: The compression cog will set ncompr to a non-negative number when it completes its work. The main cog waits in this loop until it sees that the compression cog is finished.

Lines 37–38: Print out the results. nsamps should now be zero, and ncompr should now be non-negative.

Line 40: Enter an infinite loop, doing nothing.

The output from running this program is as follows:

```
starting main
started compression cog 1
nsamps = 0, ncompr = 3
samp0 = EFCDAB, packBuf = 0 0 0
```

We have shown that we can communicate with the compression cog. How fast is it? To compare this to the Spin and PASM compression codes from the previous chapters, let's implement the compression code.

12.2.4 Compression Code in C

We will edit comprCog to include the packing. Replace the code with the code in Listing 12-7. This forms the difference between successive samples and checks the length of the difference. Depending on that length, it saves the difference as either 1, 2, or 3 bytes of packBuf. (For simplicity I haven't included the part that populates the compression code comprCodesBuf.)

Listing 12-7. Compression Code Version 2 (ch11/compr cog1.side)

```
1   /* cog code - comprCog
2    use nsamps and ncompr to signal with main cog
3      start compression when nsamps != 0
4      signal completion with ncmopr > 0
5      signal error with ncompr = 0
6      compress sampsBuf to packBuf
7      populate comprCodesBuf - NOT YET DONE
8      - args: pointer to memory space PAR - UNUSED
9      - return: none
10   */
11   void comprCog(void *p) {
12     int i, nc, nbytes, codenum, codeshift, code;
13     int diff, adiff;
14
15     while (1) {
16       if(nsamps == 0) {
17         continue; // loop continuously while nsamps is 0
18       } else {
19         // perform the compression here
20         if(nsamps > NSAMPS_MAX || nsamps < -NSAMPS_MAX) {
21           ncompr = 0; // signal error
22           nsamps = 0;
23           continue;
24         }
25         for(i=0; i< nsamps; i++) {
26           if(i ==0) { // first samp
27             memcpy(packBuf,(char *)sampsBuf, 3);
28             nc = 3;
29           } else {
30             diff = sampsBuf[i] - sampsBuf[i -1];
```

```
31              adiff = abs(diff);
32              if(adiff < TWO_BYTES) {
33                 nbytes = 1;
34              } else if(adiff < THREE_BYTES) {
35                 nbytes = 2;
36              } else {
37                 nbytes = 3;
38              }
39              // copy the correct number of bytes from diff
40              // to packBuf
41              memcpy(packBuf +nc,(char *)diff, nbytes);
42              nc += nbytes;
43           }
44        }
45        ncompr = nc; // signal completion
46        nsamps = 0;  // prevent another cycle from starting
47     }
48   }
49 }
```

Line 26–28: Here the first sample is packed. The memcpy function will copy three bytes from the memory location sampsBuf to the memory location packBuf. There are no indices on the two arrays because we are operating on the start of both arrays (sampsBuf[0] is copied to packBuf[0..2]).

Lines 30–38: Form the difference and check the length of its absolute value.

Line 41: Copy the appropriate number of bytes of the difference to packBuf.

Lines 45–46: Signal the main cog that the compression is complete by setting ncompr to the number of bytes used in packBuf. Set nsamps to zero so that the loop doesn't start again.

Add the following to the main cog:

```
1  printf(" nsamps = %d, ncompr = %d\n", nsamps, ncompr);
2  printf(" nsamps = %d, ncompr = %d\n", nsamps, ncompr);
3  printf(" sampo = %x, packBuf = %x %x %x\n", sampsBuf[0], ↵
   packBuf[0],
4  % packBuf[1], packBuf[2]);
5
6  // NEW CODE STARTS HERE >>>
7  for(i=0; i< NSAMPS_MAX; i++) {
8     sampsBuf[i] = 10000*(i +1000);
9  }
10
11  ncompr = -1;
12  t0 = CNT;
13  nsamps =128;
14  /* wait until the compression cog sets ncompr to a non -neg ↵
   number */
15  while(ncompr < 0) {
16     ;
17  }
18  t0 = CNT - t0;
19  printf(" nsamps = %d, ncompr = %d\n", nsamps, ncompr);
20  printf(" sampo = %x, packBuf = %x %x %x\n", sampsBuf[0], ↵
   packBuf[0], packBuf[1], packBuf[2]);
21  printf(" dt = %d\n", t0);
22  // NEW CODE ENDS HERE <<<
23
24
25  while (1)
26  {
27     ;
28  }
```

Lines 7–9: Initialize sampsBuf.

Lines 12–18: Time how long it takes to perform the compression of 128 samples.

The results are as follows:

```
starting main
started compression cog 1
nsamps = 0, ncompr = 3
samp0 = EFCDAB, packBuf = AB CD EF
nsamps = 0, ncompr = 384
samp0 = 989680, packBuf = 80 96 98
dt = 151600
```

Table 12-1 compares the time taken to perform the compression in different languages. Clearly the fastest language is PASM, with C being about one-fifth the speed of PASM.

Table 12-1. *Comparison of Time Taken to Compress Data Using Different Methods*

Language	Number of Counts to Compress 128 Samples
Spin code	1.5 million counts
PASM code	22,000 counts
C code (LMM)	150,000 counts

Spin is 1/10th the speed of C. In the next chapter, we will program the compression cog using Cog-C mode, where the cog code is downloaded to the cog all at once and run there. (Recall that in LMM mode the code is held on the hub, and one instruction at a time is downloaded and run on the cog.)

Because I know that I won't be using pure-C mode for the final version, I'm not going to complete the compression and decompression code—that can be an exercise for you!

12.3 Summary

The simplest multicog technique in C is the large memory model (Listing 12-8 has a template to get you started). Here, all the code for *all* the cogs is stored in the hub, along with a *kernel*, which is a small program that copies instructions to each cog as needed and executes them. The code for each cog is defined as a function that is called by the cogstart instruction.

- Set aside a chunk of memory for the stack.

- Define variables that will be shared by all the cogs.

- Define a function pureCCog whose code will be run in a separate cog (note that the external variables are available here).

- In the main function, call cogstart with the address of pureCCog. The external variables are available here too.

Listing 12-8. Template for Pure-C Code

```
1  # define STACK_SIZE_INT 100
2  # define STACK_SIZE_BYTES 4 * STACK_SIZE_INT
3
4  // This is a critical number that is difficult to estimate
5  // In a later chapter I will discuss how to set it
6  static unsigned int pureCCogStack[STACK_SIZE_INT];
7
8  // these are shared with all cogs and must be
```

```
 9  // declared `` volatile '''
10  volatile int variable1;
11  volatile int variable2;
12  volatile int dataArray[100];
13
14  // function to run in new cog - mustn't return
15  void pureCCog(void *p) {
16    while (1) {
17      ...
18      // access variable1, variable2, and dataArray[]
19    }
20  }
21
22  // the main function - mustn't return
23  int main() {
24    int pureCCogId;
25    // the calling protocol for new cogs
26    pureCCogId = cogstart (&pureCCog, NULL, pureCCogStack, ⏎
      STACK_SIZE_BYTES);
27    while (1) {
28      ...
29      // main cog can access variable1, variable2, dataArray[]
30    }
31  }
```

CHAPTER 13

Programming in Cog-C Mode

In the previous chapter, we programmed the Propeller in the large memory model where the code was all stored in hub memory and instructions were downloaded to a cog one at a time for execution. This exacts a performance penalty. If the code you want to run on a cog will fit entirely within the cog (496 longs), then you can write that code in such a way that it is copied to the cog all at once and runs on the cog natively.

© Sridhar Anandakrishnan 2018
S. Anandakrishnan, *Propeller Programming*, https://doi.org/10.1007/978-1-4842-3354-2_13

A ROTARY SNOW-PLOUGH.

Figure 13-1. *A rotary snow plough used for clearing track. From "The World's Work, Volume 1," WH Page, AW Page, Doubleday, 1901. Available for free download from Google Books* https://books.google.com/books?id=688YPNQ5HNwC.

13.1 Cog-C Mixed Mode Programming

Here we will write the main cog in the same way as in the previous chapter but will place the compression code in a separate file whose extension is cogc. This special extension will signal the compiler that the code in that file will be copied to a cog all at once.

In SimpleIDE start a new project named compr_cogc and create three files.

- compr_cogc.c is where the code for the main cog resides.

- compr.cogc is where the code for the compression cog resides.

- compr_cogc.h is a header file that contains common variable and constant declarations.

13.1.1 Main Cog Code

Listing 13-1 shows that the main cog code is similar to the code in the previous chapter with a few significant changes.

Listing 13-1. Contents of compr_cogc.c Showing Modifications from Previous Chapter

```
 1   #include <stdio.h>
 2   #include <propeller.h>
 3   // ADD THIS >>>
 4   #include " compr_cogc.h"
 5   // <<<
 6
 7   /* defines */
 8
 9   /* global variables */
10
11   // ADD THIS >>>
12   // reserved space to be passed to startComprCog
13   struct cogmem_t {
14     unsigned int stack[STACK_SIZE_BYTES >> 2];
15     volatile struct locker_t locker ;
16   } cogmem ;
17   // <<<
18
19   // shared vars
20   volatile int nsamps ;
21   volatile int ncompr ;
22   volatile int sampsBuf[NSAMPS_MAX];
23   volatile char packBuf[NSAMPS_MAX <<2]; // 128 * 4
24   volatile int comprCodesBuf[NSAMPS_MAX >>4]; // 128 / 16
25
```

```
26  // ADD THIS >>>
27  int startComprCog(volatile void *p) {
28    extern unsigned int _load_start_compr_cog [];
29    return cognew(_load_start_compr_cog, p);
30  }
31  // >>>
32
33  // DELETE THE comprCog FUNCTION
34  ...
35
36  // in main ...
37
38  ...
39
40    printf (" starting main \n");
41
42  // CHANGE TO THIS >>>
43    comprCogId = startComprCog (&cogmem.locker);
44  // <<<
45
46    if(comprCogId < 0) {
47      printf (" error starting compr cog \n");
48      while (1) {;}
49    }
50
51  ...
```

- **Lines 13–16**: Declare a structure struct cogmem_t
  {...} cogmem with two members: an array named
  stack and another structure named struct locker_t
  locker. The cogmem structure will keep the memory

for the stack and for the locker in adjacent space. The address of the locker struct will be passed to the new cog in the PAR register. Note that in this example we won't be using the locker but still define it because the kernel expects this arrangement (stack followed by the locker variables). The definition of struct locker_t is in the header file compr_cogc.h.

```
1  /* define the struct for passing data via PAR to the
   cog -- UNUSED */
2  struct locker_t {
3  };
```

- **Lines 27–30**: A function that starts the compression cog. This makes reference to the "magical" address location of _load_start_compr_cog. This form of this variable is always as follows:

  _load_start_<COGCFILENAME>_cog, where COGCFILENAME is the name of the file that contains the cog code (in our case, that file name is compr. cogc, so we put compr) in the name.

  The cognew function takes two arguments: that magical variable and the pointer p passed to the function. p points to the struct locker_t locker memory and will be placed in PAR. In this example, it is *unused*, but we still invoke it in all its messy glory so that if you ever want to use it, you know how!

- **Line 43**: We start the cog by calling the startComprCog function. It takes one variable, which is the address of the struct locker_t variable in the cogmem structure: &cogmem.locker.

When the main cog runs, it will call comprCogStart with the address of the start of the locker memory block (&cogmem.locker). Remember, the & operator returns the address of the variable, and cogmem.locker refers to the variable locker in the struct cogmem. Yes, I know it is messy, but if you copy this pattern slavishly, it should work.

13.1.2 Compression Cog-C Code

The compression code is placed in its own file, compr.cogc, as shown in Listing 13-2. (You must have the cogc extension.) Whatever name you choose for this file is what shows up in the cognew command _load_start_compr_cog.

Listing 13-2. Contents of compr.cogc

```
1  #include "compr_cogc.h"
2  #include <propeller.h>
3
4  // shared vars
5  extern volatile int nsamps ;
6  extern volatile int ncompr ;
7  extern volatile int sampsBuf[NSAMPS_MAX];
8  extern volatile char packBuf[NSAMPS_MAX <<2]; // 128 * 4
9  extern volatile int comprCodesBuf[NSAMPS_MAX >>4]; // 128 / 16
10
11 /* cog code - compr
12    use nsamps and ncompr to signal with main cog
13      start compression when nsamps != 0
14      signal completion with ncmopr > 0
15      signal error with ncompr = 0
16    compress sampsBuf to packBuf
17    populate comprCodesBuf
```

```
18     - args : pointer to memory space PAR - UNUSED
19     - return : none
20   */
21
22   void main (struct locker_t *p) {
23     int i, nc, nbytes, codenum, codeshift, code ;
24     int diff, adiff ;
25
26     while (1) {
27       if (nsamps == 0) {
28         continue ; // loop continuously while nsamps is 0
29       } else {
30
31         // perform the compression here
32         if (nsamps > NSAMPS_MAX || nsamps < -NSAMPS_MAX) {
33           ncompr = 0; // signal error
34           nsamps = 0;
35           continue ;
36         }
37         for(i=0; i< nsamps ; i++) {
38           if(i ==0) { // first samp
39             memcpy (packBuf, (char *) sampsBuf, 3);
40             nc = 3;
41           } else {
42             diff = sampsBuf[i] - sampsBuf[i -1];
43             adiff = abs(diff);
44             if (adiff < TWO_BYTES) {
45               nbytes = 1;
46               code = CODE08 ;
47             } else if (adiff < THREE_BYTES) {
48               nbytes = 2;
49               code = CODE16 ;
```

```
50              } else {
51                 nbytes = 3;
52                 code = CODE24 ;
53              }
54              // copy the correct number of bytes from diff
55              // to packBuf
56              memcpy (packBuf +nc, (char *) diff, nbytes);
57              nc += nbytes ;
58           }
59        }
60       ncompr = nc; // signal completion
61       nsamps = 0; // prevent another cycle from starting
62     }
63   }
64 }
```

- **Lines 5–9**: These are variables that are shared between the main cog and this cog. The extern qualifier tells the compiler not to reserve new space but that this variable has been defined in another file. From now on, any reference to, for example, nsamps will reference the same variable as in the main cog (where it was originally defined). The volatile qualifier tells the compiler that even if it looks like this variable isn't used, don't optimize it away. It could be modified in, for example, the main cog.

- **Line 22**: The cog code is placed in its own main function that should never return. It takes one argument, a pointer to a memory block (this is the equivalent of PAR). In this example, this is *unused* because we prefer to use the shared variables.

Everything else is the same as in the previous chapter.

13.1.3 Header File compr_cogc.h

Listing 13-3 shows the contents of compr_cogc.h.

Listing 13-3. Contents of compr_cogc.h

```
 1  // size of stack in bytes
 2  #define STACK_SIZE_BYTES 200
 3  // compression constants
 4  #define NSAMPS_MAX 128
 5  #define CODE08 0b01
 6  #define CODE16 0b10
 7  #define CODE24 0b11
 8  #define TWO_BYTES 0x7F // any diff values greater than this ↵
                          are 2 bytes
 9  #define THREE_BYTES 0 x7FF // diff valus greater than this ↵
                          are 3 bytes
10
11  /* define the struct for passing data via PAR to the ↵
    cog -- UNUSED */
12  struct locker_t {
13  };
```

This is the front matter that is used by both the main cog and the compression cog (both have the line #include "compr_cogc.h"). The struct locker_t declaration is empty because it is a placeholder that we don't use.

13.1.4 Running the Cog-C Code

Make sure that you have chosen LMM Main Ram as your memory model on the Project Options tab. (Even though you have chosen LMM, because the compr.cogc file has a .cogc extension, it will be compiled in Cog-C mode and copied to a new cog and run in that cog natively.)

```
starting main
started compression cog 1
done... nsamps = 0, ncompr = 3
samp0 = EFCDAB, packBuf = AB CD EF
nsamps = 0, ncompr = 384
samp0 = 989680, packBuf = 80 96 98
dt = 42064
```

Let's compare the running speed to the other ways of compressing 128 longs. See Table 13-1.

Table 13-1. *Comparison of Compression Speeds with Cog-C Mode Added*

Language	Number of Counts to Compress 128 Samples (Smaller Is Better)
Spin code	1.5 million counts
PASM code	22,000 counts
C code (LMM only)	150,000 counts
Cog-C mode	42,000 counts

Clearly, programming in Cog-C mode improves speed by about a factor of three to four over LMM C mode. As you can see, PASM is still the fastest method, but Cog-C is no slouch!

13.2 Summary

We can start a new cog that is running in *Cog-C* mode, in which the C code
is compiled to PASM and copied in its entirety to a cog and run there. Of
course, the compiled code must be less than 496 longs (the size of cog
memory).

- In the main file, we must set aside a chunk of memory
  for the stack and the "locker" (struct cogmem_t); a
  template for the main file is in Listing 13-4.

- Define shared variables that will be available to all cogs
  (volatile int x).

- Define a function that starts the cog (int
  startMyCogC(...)).

- Create a file named myCogC.cogc that contains the code
  to be loaded to the new cog; a template for the cog-C
  file is in Listing 13-5.

- In the main file, call the startMyCogC function.

- In the .cogc file, refer to the shared variables using
  extern volatile int x so the cog can use them.

Listing 13-4. Contents of main.c for Cog-C Mixed Mode

```
1  // in main .c
2  #define STACK_SIZE_INTS 50
3
4  // put this in a mycogc .h file (common to this file and ↵
       mycogc .cogc)
5  // #include " mycogc .h"
6  struct cogmem_t {
7    unsigned int stack[STACK_SIZE_INTS];
8    volatile struct locker_t locker ;
```

```
 9  };
10
11  // declare the cog memory for the new cog
12  // there must be a different memory space for each cog
13  struct cogmem_t myCogCMem ;
14
15  // shared with all cogs
16  volatile int variable1 ;
17  volatile int variable2 ;
18  volatile int dataArray[100];
19
20  // start the new cog ...
21  int startMyCogC(volatile void * parptr) {
22    extern unsigned int _load_start_myCogC_cog[];
23    return cognew(_load_start_myCogC_cog, parptr);
24  }
25
26  int main () {
27    int myCogCId ;
28    // start the new cog . the address of locker is passed to
29    // the cognew command as parptr
30    myCogCId = startMyCogC(&myCogCMem . locker);
31  ...
32    while (1) {
33      ...
34      // access variable1, variable2, dataArray [] in main cog
35    }
36  }
```

Listing 13-5. Contents of the .cogc File

```
1   // contents of myCogC .cogc
2
3   // put this in a mycogc .h file and
4   // # include " mycogc .h"
5   struct cogmem_t {
6     unsigned int stack [STACK_SIZE_INTS];
7     volatile struct locker_t locker ;
8   };
9
10  // any variables declared in another file
11  // must be set as `` extern '' so that the
12  // compiler knows where to find them.
13  extern volatile int variable1 ;
14  extern volatile int variable2 ;
15  extern volatile int dataArray [100];
16
17  // the code that will run in the new cog
18  // must be small enough to fit in 496 longs.
19  // the compiler will complain if it is too big
20  void main(struct locker_t *p)
21    while (1) {
22      ...
23      // access variable1, variable2, and dataArray [] in 2nd cog
24    }
25  }
```

CHAPTER 14

Programming with C and PASM

In this chapter, we will look at the combination of using C for the main cog (and any other cogs that are not required to be fast) and PASM for the critical cog that must run as fast as possible. For this mode, we must use the PAR method of passing variables between the main cog and the compression cog (in pure-C programming, we use shared variables, but that isn't possible here). Hitching together fast and slow components has been done before - see Figure 14-1 for an example!

© Sridhar Anandakrishnan 2018
S. Anandakrishnan, *Propeller Programming*, https://doi.org/10.1007/978-1-4842-3354-2_14

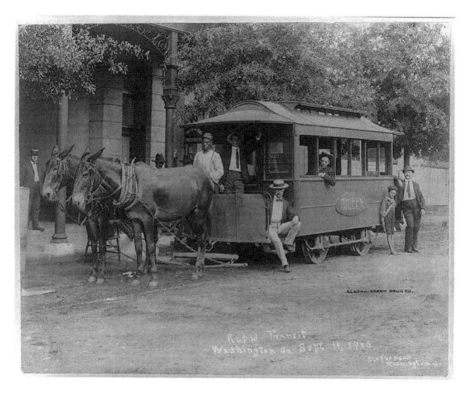

Figure 14-1. *Rapid Transit, Washington, GA 1903. Photographer JW Stephenson. Library of Congress archives (http://www.loc.gov/pictures/item/2012646774).*

In summary, we will do the following:

- In the C program, we will create a block of memory (using a struct) that contains the variables we want to pass to the PASM cog. Because we use a struct, the variables are in contiguous memory.

- We create a Spin/PASM file that has one Spin method (START) that calls cognew to start a PASM cog. The address of the struct is passed to this cog in PAR.

- Now the C program and the PASM cog can interact through the variables in the struct.

14.1 Compression with C and PASM

Create a new project in SimpleIDE called `compr_c_pasm` and create two
files: `compr_c_pasm.c` and `compr.spin`.

14.1.1 C Code for Main Cog

Listing 14-1 shows the contents of the PASM file.

Listing 14-1. Contents of ch12/compr_c_pasm.c

```
1   /* libraries */
2   #include <stdio.h>
3   #include <propeller.h>
4
5   /* defines */
6
7   // compression constants
8   #define NSAMPS_MAX 128
9
10  /* global variables */
11  // reserved space to be passed to startComprPASMCog
12  volatile struct locker_t {
13    int nsamps ;
14    int ncompr ;
15    int *psampsBuf ;
16    unsigned char *ppackBuf ;
17    int *pcomprCodesBuf ;
18  } locker ;
19
20  volatile int sampsBuf[NSAMPS_MAX];
21  volatile unsigned char packBuf[NSAMPS_MAX <<2]; // 128 * 4
```

```
22  volatile int comprCodesBuf[NSAMPS_MAX >>4]; // 128 / 16
23
24  int startComprPASMCog(unsigned int * parptr) {
25    extern unsigned int binary_compr_dat_start[];
26    return cognew(binary_compr_dat_start, parptr);
27  }
28
29
30  /* main cog - initializes variables and starts new cogs.
31   * don 't exit - start infinite loop as the last thing.
32   */
33  int main(void)
34  {
35    int comprCogId = -1;
36    int i;
37    unsigned int t0;
38
39    locker.nsamps = 0;
40    locker.ncompr = -1;
41    locker.psampsBuf = sampsBuf ;
42    locker.ppackBuf = packBuf ;
43    locker.pcomprCodesBuf = comprCodesBuf ;
44
45    printf (" starting main \n");
46
47    comprCogId = startComprPASMCog (&locker);
48    if(comprCogId < 0) {
49      printf (" error starting compr cog \n");
50      while (1) {;}
51    }
52
```

```
53    printf(" started compression cog %d\n", comprCogId);
54
55    /* start the compression cog by setting nsamps to 1 */
56    sampsBuf [0] = 0 xEFCDAB ;
57    locker.nsamps = 1; //= cogmem.locker.nsamps = 1;
58
59    /* wait until the compression cog sets ncompr to a
      non -neg number */
60    while(locker.ncompr < 0) {
61      ;
62    }
63
64    printf(" done ... nsamps = %d, ncompr = %d\n",
      locker.nsamps, locker.ncompr);
65    printf(" samp0 = %x, packBuf = %x %x %x\n", sampsBuf
      [0], packBuf [0], packBuf [1], packBuf [2]) ;
66
67    while (1)
68    {
69      ;// do nothing
70    }
71  }
```

- **Lines 12–18**: Declare a structure that contains all the variables to be passed to the PASM cog. By placing them in a struct, you ensure that they will remain contiguous and in order. The PASM cog finds variables by knowing their address relative to the start of the memory location passed to it in PAR. So, the PASM cog expects nsamps to be at the start of that memory block and ncompr to be 4 bytes past that.

- **Lines 15–17**: Here we place the addresses for the three arrays. psampsBuf is the address of sampsBuf and so on. Pointers in C are 4 bytes long, so the three pointers are at the correct locations that the PASM cog expects. The expression int *p says that p is a pointer to an int array.

- **Lines 20–21**: The arrays themselves are declared here. They are also qualified to be volatile so the compiler won't inadvertently remove them.

- **Lines 24–27**: This is the function that starts the PASM cog. It has a "magic" invocation as well. binary_compr_dat_start is the address in memory of the code to be written to the cog. The variable has the form binary_<PASMFILENAME>_dat_start, where PASMFILENAME has a .spin extension (in our case, compr.spin).

- **Lines 39–43**: The lockers are populated. A member of a struct is accessed via locker.nsamps, and so on. The address of an array, such as sampsBuf[], can be obtained by simply mentioning the name of the array, as in locker.psampsBuf = sampsBuf and so on.

- **Line 47**: Here we call the function that starts the cog and pass the address of the beginning of the locker: &locker. The address of the first member of a struct is the same as the address of the struct variable; thus, the address of nsamps is given by &locker (remember, the & operator returns the address of the variable).

14.1.2 PASM Code

The PASM code that will run in the new cog is placed in a file with the
.spin extension (see Listing 14-2). The file name will appear in the extern
variable binary_compr_dat_start in the main code.

Listing 14-2. Contents of compr.spin

```
1
2   PUB START (locker)
3     cognew (@STEIM, locker)
4
5
6   DAT 'steim
7   ''
8   ''
9
10  STEIM org 0
11    ' copy the param addresses
12    mov _cnsPtr, par
13    mov _cncomprPtr, par
14    add _cncomprPtr, #4
15  ...
```

- **Lines 2–3**: Define a public method named START that
  calls the Spin method cognew. As in regular Spin code,
  this has two arguments: the address of the PASM code
  we want to run (in this case @STEIM) and the memory
  location to place in PAR (in this case locker). When the
  main C cog starts the cog with the following, the memory
  location parptr is passed to this START method and then
  passed on to the Spin cognew method here.

  cognew(binary_compr_dat_start, parptr)

273

- **Lines 6–15**: This code is lifted directly from the PASM
  code in Chapter 9.

Running this code results in compression speeds almost identical to
the PASM case (as it should, this is really the same code running in the
same way). See Table 14-1.

Table 14-1. *Comparison of Compression Speeds with Cog-C
Mode Added*

Language	Number of Counts to Compress 128 Samples (Smaller Is Better)
Spin code	1.5 million counts
PASM code	22,000 counts
C code (LMM only)	150,000 counts
Cog-C mode	42,000 counts
C and PASM code	22,000 counts

14.2 Summary

You can start a pure-PASM cog if, for example, you have some tested and
fast code that you want to reuse. To do so, you must have two files: one in C
and one in Spin and PASM. The C program will create a block of memory
(in the hub). That memory location is passed to the Spin method, which
passes it to the PASM cog.

The main C file in Listing 14-3 has a template for creating the memory
(struct locker_t ... locker;) and calling the Spin method START in
the file fastCog.spin (Listing 14-4): cognew(binary_fastCog_dat_start,
parptr);.

Listing 14-3. Template for C/PASM: C File

```
1   // Contents of main.c
2
3   // the address of the locker struct is equal to the address of the
4   // first field in the struct. That address is passed to the
5   // PASM cog in PAR. The PASM cog will determine the addresses
6   // of the other variables; they are in consecutive ↵
        memory locations
7   struct locker_t {
8     int variable1 ;
9     int variable2 ;
10    int * array ; // this is a pointer to an array
11  } locker ;
12
13  // start the cog
14  int startFastCog(unsigned int * parptr) {
15    extern unsigned int binary_fastCog_dat_start [];
16    return cognew(binary_fastCog_dat_start, parptr);
17  }
18
19  // this array is only available to the main cog
20  // in order to pass it to the PASM cog, copy it 's
21  // address to the locker
22  volatile int dataArray [100];
23
24  int main () {
25    int fastCogId ;
26    locker.variable1 =42; // populate the locker
27    locker.variable2 =12;
```

```
28    locker.array = dataArray ; // copy the address of the ↵
                                    array to the locker
29    // start the PASM cog
30    fastCogId = startFastCog (& locker);
31
32    // from here on, locker.variable1, etc may be modified ↵
         by fastCog
33    while (1) {
34      ;
35    }
36  }
37  // main.c ends here
```

The Spin/PASM file (Listing 14-4) has a single Spin method (START) whose argument is the address of memory (in the hub) that we want to share with the PASM cog. This address is used as the second argument to the cognew call that launches the PASM cog (and, therefore, that address is placed in PAR). In the PASM cog, we can modify memory in the hub that the C program is, presumably, interested in.

Listing 14-4. Template for C/PASM: PASM File

```
1  ' the contents of fastCog.spin
2  ' locker is the address of the " locker " variable from ↵
   the main cog
3  PUB START(locker)
4    cognew(@FASTCOG, locker)
5
6  DAT 'fastcog
7  FASTCOG org 0
8    mov _var1Ptr, par ' par contains the address of locker, which
9                      ' is also the address of the first ↵
                       field, variable1
```

```
10    mov _var2Ptr, par
11    mov _arrayPtr, par
12    add _var2Ptr, #4 ' variable2 is 4 bytes after variable1
13    add _arrayPtr, #8 ' the * address * of the array is 8 ↵
      bytes after variable1
14    ...
15    ' and we 're off to the races
16    rdlong _cVar1, _var1Ptr ' get C's locker.variable1
17    add _cVar1, #42        ' do something
18    wrlong _cVar1, _var1Ptr ' write it back
19
20    ...
21  _var1Ptr res 1
22  _var2Ptr res 1
23  _arrayPtr res 1
24  _cVar1 res 1
25  FIT 496
26  'fastCog.spin ends here
```

CHAPTER 15

Hardware I/O with C

We can work with the hardware in C (setting and reading pins and counters) in one of three ways: using direct calls to the registers (INA, DIRA, etc.), using the simpletools utility library, and using C code and *injecting* PASM code in critical sections. This is known as *inline assembler* mode.

Let's begin with the simpler library method and then move on to the others.

We will write an SPI master and slave and put each in its own cog (see Section 7.1 for details on SPI). The SPI slave stands in for a data acquisition device that produces data. The SPI master is the interface to that "device." The main cog works only with the SPI master to receive data and process, print, or store it.

© Sridhar Anandakrishnan 2018
S. Anandakrishnan, *Propeller Programming*, https://doi.org/10.1007/978-1-4842-3354-2_15

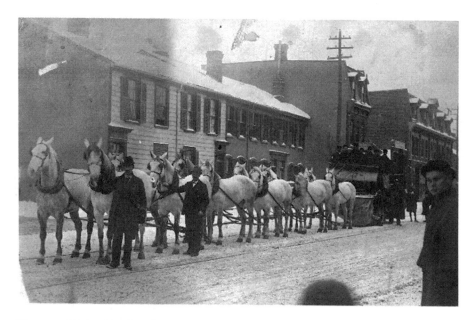

Figure 15-1. *Twelve-horse team pulling snow sweeper. Toronto, 1891. From City of Toronto archives. Image in public domain.* `https://commons.wikimedia.org/wiki/File%3ATwelve_horse_ team_pulling_snow_sweeper.jpg.`

15.1 Referencing Hardware in C

By including the propeller.h library, the following functions and variables are available (unlike Spin and PASM, these are case-sensitive):

- DIRA sets the direction of the 32 I/O pins. If a bit *N* is a 1, then that pin will be an output. All cogs have their own copy of the DIRA register. More than one cog can set a pin as output, and if any of those cogs drives the pin high (by setting that bit in the OUTA register), then that pin will go high.

- OUTA sets the value of pin *N* to either high or low by setting the bit in that position to 1 or 0, respectively. The pin itself will be driven high or low only if the associated bit in the DIRA register is a 1.

- INA (read-only) reflects the state of the pins. If the pin is high, the bit in that position will be a 1.

- CNT (read-only) is the value of the internal counter, which increments once each clock cycle.

- waitpne and waitpeq wait for the state of the inputs to match a requested state (see Chapter 7).

- waitcnt is like Spin's waitcnt; it takes one argument, target, and the cog is paused until the counter equals the target value. waitcnt2 is like the PASM waitcnt, with two arguments: a target value and a delta value. The cog is paused until the target count is reached. The target is incremented by delta for repeated and reliable delays.

- locknew, lockret, lockset, and lockclr are all as in Spin and PASM.

- C has some bitwise operators such as AND (&), OR (|), and XOR (^), and shift left (<<) and shift right (>>). It is missing the rotate left and right operators of Spin and PASM, the reverse bits operator, and the arithmetic shift operator. There are functions for performing those operations in C (see http://graphics.stanford. edu/~seander/bithacks.html).

15.2 simpletools Library

By including the simpletools library (with #include <simpletools.h>), you have access to a number of functions that simplify hardware manipulations. However, the authors of simpletools warn that it is best to use these functions in straight C code (LMM-only mode). This is because the library is too large to fit in a cog (remember, cog memory is limited to 496 longs). The library consists of a number of functions and variables.[1]

For example, set a pin with high(N), low(N), or toggle(N). Get the value of an input pin with v = input(pin). There are more-complex ways to set the direction and get the state of a single pin or of multiple pins. There are functions to use the I2C and SPI protocols as well as a full duplex serial port.

Flashing an LED on the QuickStart board (from http://learn. parallax.com/tutorials) is self-explanatory, as shown in Listing 15-1.

Listing 15-1. Hello Blinky: Using simpletools.h to Toggle an LED

```
1   #include " simpletools.h"
2   #define LED0 16 # pin number for LED0 on Quickstart board.
3   int main ()
4   {
5     while (1) {
6       high (LED0);
7       pause (100) ; // Wait 100 ms (1/10 sec)
8       low (LED0);
9       pause (100) ;
10    }
11  }
```

---

[1]See SimpleIDE/Learn/Simple%20Libraries/Utility/libsimpletools/ Documentation%20simpletools%20Library.html; the SimpleIDE folder is in the Documents folder.

15.3 Using the Registers Directly

Particularly in Cog-C mode or whenever speed or flexibility is an issue, you will want to address the input and output registers directly.

15.3.1 Set a Pin

Set a bit, as shown in Listing 15-2.

Listing 15-2. Setting a Pin in C Using the OUTA Register

```
1   #include <propeller.h>
2   #define LED0 16   // pin number for LED0 on Quickstart board.
3   #define LED0MASK (1U << LED0)
4   int main () {
5     unsigned int delayTime = CLKFREQ /2;
6     OUTA = 0;  // set all bits to zero
7     DIRA |= LED0MASK ; // set pin 16 to output
8     while (1) {
9       OUTA ^= LED0MASK ;  // toggle pin 16
10      waitcnt (CNT + delayTime);
11    }
12  }
```

- **Line 3**: Create a *mask* where bit 16 is high and the others are low.

- **Lines 6–7**: Set the output register to all 0s and then set the output direction for pin 16 to 1. The expression DIRA |= LED0MASK will perform a bitwise OR of the DIRA register and the LED0MASK and assign the result back to DIRA. The result is that bit 16 in DIRA is set to 1 (output).

- **Line 9**: Perform an exclusive OR of OUTA and LEDOMASK. In an exclusive OR, compare the two arguments bit by bit, and return a 1 if and only if one of the two bits is 1. If both are 0 or both are 1, then the bit is set to 0. Thus, as bit 16 of LEDOMASK is always 1, if bit 16 of OUTA is 0, then the exclusive OR will set bit 16 of OUTA to 1 (1^0 = 1). If bit 16 of OUTA is 1, then the exclusive OR will set it to 0 (1^1 = 0).

15.3.2 Read a Pin

The QuickStart board doesn't have a button, but it has a touchpad. Here you set the touchpad pin high and read its value after a short time. If you are touching the pad, then the conduction of your skin will quickly force the pin low. If you aren't touching it, then the pin will remain high for a long time (it will eventually decay to low because there is a large resistor to ground that will eventually pull it low).

In Listing 15-3 we toggle the LED every time we touch pad 0.

Listing 15-3. Toggle an LED Using Registers in C

```
1   #include <propeller.h>
2   #define LEDO 16  // pin number for LEDO on Quickstart board.
3   #define LEDOMask (1U << LEDO)
4   #define PADO 0  // pin number for PADO on Quickstart board.
5   #define PADOMask (1U << PADO)
6   int main ()
7   {
8     DIRA = 0;
9     OUTA = 0;
10    DIRA |= LEDOMask ;
```

```
11    OUTA |= LEDOMask ; // illuminate LED0
12    while (1) {
13      waitcnt (CNT + CLKFREQ /10) ; // don 't do this too ↩
        quickly ...
14      DIRA |= PADOMask ; // set to output
15      OUTA |= PADOMask ; // set pad0 high
16      DIRA ^= PADOMask ; // set pad0 back to input
17      waitcnt (CNT + CLKFREQ /1000) ;
18      if (INA & PADOMask) // still high - no touch
19        continue ;
20      OUTA ^= LEDOMask ;
21    }
22  }
```

- **Lines 8–11**: Set the output state register OUTA and the direction register DIRA to illuminate the LED.

- **Lines 13–15**: Set the pad 0 pin to output, raise it high, and set it back to input.

- **Lines 16–19**: Wait 1ms and check the value of the pad 0 pin. The INA register bit 0 will reflect the value of pin 0. Thus, if pad 0 is high (not touching the touchpad), then bit 0 of INA is high, the AND will return TRUE, and the loop will continue without changing the LED. If pad 0 is low (you touched the touchpad), the AND will return FALSE and the next statement toggling the LED will be executed instead.

15.4 Implementing SPI in Cog-C

Let's implement the SPI protocol in Cog-C. The main cog will start two cogs: an SPI master and an SPI slave. The master cog will request a long of data from the slave and store it to a shared array. The slave cog will wait for a request and transmit a number (our fake data is zero the first time and increments by one for each request).

In SPI, communication is controlled by the master, which asserts (lowers) the chip select (CS) line and then transmits a clock (CLK). The master reads the MISO (master in, slave out) line at the rising edge of the clock (see Figure 15-2 for an example). The slave watches for the CS line to go low and must place data on the MISO line before the rising edge of each clock cycle. We will use 32-bit wide words, with the most significant bit (MSB) transmitted first.

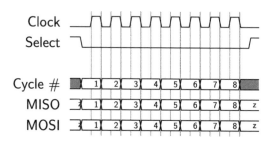

Figure 15-2. *SPI timing diagram for the case when the clock starts out low (CPOL=0) and the data is required to be valid on a rising edge (CPHA=0)*

15.5 Goals of This Chapter

In this chapter we will set all the necessary lines at the right times (and monitor and read them in the slave). We will exercise a number of ways of setting and reading particular bits in a number. In the next chapter, we will replace some of the "bit-twiddling" code with *inline PASM* to speed things up.

The structure of our project is as follows: a main cog will start two other cogs that communicate via SPI. The spiSlave stands in for a hardware device (for example, an analog to digital converter [ADC]) that produces data. The spiMaster will read data from the spiSlave and store it in the array data, which will be read by the main cog.

The main/controller cog and the SPI master cog must coordinate their access to the data array. We will use a *lock* to signal between main and spiMaster that the data array is either being filled with data by spiMaster or ready for processing by main (see Figure 15-3 for a diagram illustrating this process).

Create a new project called spi-c with four files: spi-c.c, spi-c.h, spiMaster.cogc, and spiSlave.cogc.

Because the SPI master and slave are .cogc files, they will be placed entirely in cog memory.

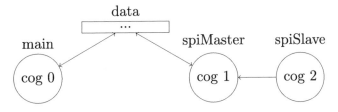

Figure 15-3. *Structure of the SPI program*

15.5.1 Main Cog (Controller)

The main cog will control the other cogs. It will launch the SPI master and slave and process the data that the master receives from the slave. The data will be stored in a shared memory array called data[]. To ensure that the main cog knows when the master is done populating the data array, we use a lock (semaphore). Listing 15-4 has the contents of the main file, which will start up two cogs (the master and the slave) and print the contents of the data array once the master has received all the data from the slave.

Listing 15-4. Contents of Main File spi-c.c

```
1   #include <stdio.h>
2   #include <propeller.h>
3   #include "c-hw.h"
4
5   struct cogmem_t {
6     unsigned int stack [50];
7     volatile struct locker_t locker ;
8   };
9
10  /* reserve memory for spimaster cog and spislave cog */
11  struct cogmem_t mcogmem ; // master
12  struct cogmem_t scogmem ; // slave
13
14  /* functions to start cogc cogs */
15  int startSPIMaster (volatile void *p) {
16    extern unsigned int _load_start_spiMaster_cog [];
17    return cognew (_load_start_spiMaster_cog, p);
18  }
19  int startSPISlave (volatile void *p) {
20    extern unsigned int _load_start_spiSlave_cog [];
21    return cognew (_load_start_spiSlave_cog, p);
22  }
23
24  /* shared memory with cogs */
25  volatile unsigned char masterSem ;
26  volatile int data [NSAMPS_MAX];
27
28  int main ()
29  {
30    int masterCogId, slaveCogId, i;
```

```
31    unsigned int t0;
32
33    masterSem = locknew ();
34    while (lockset (masterSem)) {;} // obtain lock
35
36    /* start both cogs */
37    masterCogId = startSPIMaster (&mcogmem.locker);
38    slaveCogId = startSPISlave (&scogmem.locker);
39
40    printf (" master id = %d slave id = %d sem = %d\n", ↩
      masterCogId, slaveCogId, masterSem);
41    t0 = CNT ;
42
43    lockclr (masterSem); // release lock, spimaster obtains lock
44    // wait for spimaster to release lock,
45    while (lockset (masterSem)) {;}
46    t0 = CNT - t0;
47    printf (" Time to read 128 longs = %d\n", t0);
48
49    // process array
50    for(i=0;i< NSAMPS_MAX ;i++)
51      printf ("i=%d data =%x\n", i, data [i]);
52
53    DIRA |= LEDOMask ;
54
55    while (1)
56    {
57      OUTA ^= LEDOMask ;
58    }
59  }
```

- **Lines 5–12**: We define a struct cogmem_t with space for the stack and a dummy entry for the locker (the PAR locker is unused because we use shared global memory). We declare and reserve memory for the two cogs as mcogmem and scogmem.

- **Lines 15–22**: Functions to start the master and slave cogs.

- **Lines 25–26**: Shared global memory. The masterSem is where the lock (semaphore) is stored that will be used by the main cog and the SPI master to control access to the data array. The data array is simply, and with great originality, named data[].

- **Lines 33–34**: Create a new semaphore and obtain the lock in the main cog. Thus, when we start the SPI master cog, it will sit idle attempting to obtain the lock.

- **Lines 37–38**: Start the two SPI cogs.

- **Line 43**: Release the Kraken. Upon main releasing the lock, the SPI master will obtain it, which will start a data acquisition cycle. During this time, the main cog should not touch the data array.

- **Line 45**: Continuously attempt to obtain the lock. Only once the SPI master has completed a data acquisition cycle will it release the lock, allowing the main cog to proceed beyond here.

- **Lines 50–51**: "Process" the data; print it out.

The header file (Listing 15-5) contains the pin definitions for the SPI transfer as well as a dummy locker definition (we don't use the PAR locker; rather, we prefer to use shared memory).

Listing 15-5. Contents of Header File spi-c.h

```
1   #define NSAMPS_MAX 128
2
3   #define LED0 16
4   #define LED0Mask (1U << LED0)
5
6   #define CS 10
7   #define CLK 11
8   #define MOSI 12
9   #define MISO 13
10  #define CSMask (1U << CS)
11  #define CLKMask (1U << CLK)
12  #define MOSIMask (1U << MOSI)
13  #define MISOMask (1U << MISO)
14
15  struct locker_t {
16  };
```

15.5.2 SPI Master

The SPI master (Listing 15-6) begins by setting the SPI pins CS, CLK, and MOSI as outputs. The CS line idles high and is active low, so set it high before setting it as an output. Next, obtain the lock, which starts an acquisition cycle. Acquisition consists of lowering the CS line and then clocking out 32 cycles on the CLK line. At each rising edge of CLK, read the value of the MISO and shift it into val. Finally, place val into data[]. After NSAMPS_MAX acquisitions, release the lock.

Listing 15-6. Contents of spiMaster.cogc

```
 1  #include "c-hw.h"
 2  #include <propeller.h>
 3
 4  extern unsigned char masterSem ;
 5  extern int data [NSAMPS_MAX];
 6  void main (struct locker_t *p) {
 7    int i, j, val, bit ;
 8    int clkwidth =50;
 9
10    // init SPI pins
11    OUTA = 0;
12    OUTA |= CSMask ; // preset CS high
13    DIRA = 0;
14    DIRA |= CSMask | CLKMask | MOSIMask ; // set to outputs
15
16    while (1) {
17      while (lockset (masterSem)) { // wait to obtain lock
18        ;
19      }
20      // read from spi and write to data []
21      for (i=0; i< NSAMPS_MAX ; i++) {
22        OUTA ^= CSMask ; // lower cs
23        val = 0;
24        for (j =31; j >=0; j --) {
25          waitcnt (CNT + clkwidth); // wait
26          OUTA ^= CLKMask ; // raise clock
27
28          // get value of miso pin and put in low bit
29          bit = (INA & MISOMask) >> MISO ;
30          // shift bit into val
```

```
31        val |= bit << j;
32        waitcnt (CNT + clkwidth);
33        OUTA ^= CLKMask ; // lower clock
34      }
35    data [i] = val ;
36    OUTA ^= CSMask ; // raise cs
37    waitcnt (CNT +3* clkwidth);
38    }
39
40    lockclr (masterSem); // release lock
41  }
42 }
```

- **Lines 4–5**: The shared global memory is referenced with the extern keyword.

- **Line 8**: We include a short delay between clock transitions so that the SPI master and slave have enough time to read and write the bit. This is generally specified by the device. Here I set it as low as I could and not corrupt the data (I did this by trial and error).

- **Lines 11–14**: Set CS high by setting that bit of OUTA to 1. Set CS, CLK, and MOSI as outputs by setting those bits of DIRA to 1. (MOSI—master out, slave in—is unused here but could be used to transmit data to the slave.)

- **Line 17**: Wait here until the lock is obtained. masterSem is shared from the main cog.

- **Lines 21–38**: Acquire NSAMPS_MAX samples.

- **Line 22**: Lower the CS line by performing an exclusive OR of OUTA with CSMask. We already set the CS bit of OUTA high, so the XOR will lower it.

- **Lines 24–24**: Loop over the 32 bits, high bit to low bit.

- **Lines 26 and 29**: Raise the CLK line and read the value of MISO pin in the INA register. Shift it right by MISO places so that the variable bit contains either a 0 or a 1 in the lowest bit location.

- **Line 31**: Now shift the low bit of the variable bit left by 31, 30, …, 0 bits into val.

- **Line 33**: Lower the clock line and repeat.

- **Lines 35 and 36**: Place the number val into data[] and raise the CS line, ending the acquisition of the i-th number.

- **Line 37**: Introduce a delay between acquisition requests so the SPI slave can prepare for the next request.

- **Line 40**: Once all NSAMPS_MAX samples have been acquired, release the lock back to the main cog for it to process the data.

15.5.3 SPI Slave (Simulated Data Producing Device)

The SPI slave (Listing 15-7) stands in for a data acquisition device or digitizer. It will wait for the CS line to go low and then place the MSB of its "data" on the MISO line. Once it sees the CLK line go high and low, it is free to put the next bit on the MISO line. Rinse and repeat 32 times.

Listing 15-7. Contents of File spiSlave.cogc

```
1   #include "c-hw.h"
2   #include <propeller.h>
3
4   static _COGMEM int val ;
5   static _COGMEM int j;
6   static _COGMEM int bit ;
7   void main(struct locker_t *p) {
8     int i=0;
9     DIRA = 0;
10    OUTA = 0;
11    DIRA |= MISOMask ;
12
13    i=0;
14    while (1) {
15      val = i;
16      waitpeq(CSMask, CSMask);
17      waitpne(CSMask, CSMask);
18      for (j =31; j >=0; j --) {
19        bit = (val >> j) & 0x01; // get jth bit
20        OUTA ^= (- bit ^ OUTA) & MISOMask ; // set miso pin ↵
          of outa to bit
21        waitpeq(CLKMask, CLKMask); // wait for rising clock ...
22        waitpne(CLKMask, CLKMask); // and then falling clock
23      }
24      OUTA &= ! MISOMask ; // lower miso line
25      i++;
26    }
27  }
```

- **Lines 4–6**: `static _COGMEM int val` will ensure that the variable `val` is stored in cog memory (like a `val long 0` expression in PASM) rather than being stored in hub memory. This will speed up use of that variable because hub access is slower than cog memory access.

- **Line 11**: Set the `MISO` line as an output.

- **Lines 16–17**: Ensure that the `CS` line is high and then that it is low. This high-to-low transition signals the start of an SPI data transmission cycle.

- **Lines 19–20**: `val` is the value to be transmitted to the SPI master. Get the j-th bit (starting at the most significant bit).

- **Line 20**: This mysterious concoction sets the bit in `OUTA` that corresponds to the high bit of `MISOMask` to the value of `bit`. I stole it from `http://graphics.stanford.edu/~seander/bithacks.html`.

- **Line 21**: Wait for the rising clock. In the previous line I set the `MISO` line to bit `j` of `val`, and on the rising clock the SPI master will read that bit value.

- **Line 22**: Wait until the clock goes low. The `MISO` line must hold the j-th bit throughout the time the clock is high to allow the SPI master time to read it. Once the master lowers the `CLK` line, the slave is free to move on and put the next bit on the `MISO` line.

- **Line 24**: After all 32 bits have been transmitted, clear the `MISO` line (which is not strictly necessary).

15.5.4 Running the SPI Code

Let's run the code.

```
master id = 1 slave id = 2 sem = 1
Time to read 128 longs = 623664
i=0 data=0
i=1 data=1
i=2 data=2

... lines deleted

i=127 data=7F
```

We successfully acquired 128 32-bit samples and processed them. It took about 623,000 counts, or 7.8ms, to acquire those samples (this board has an 80MHz clock). Thus, the data transfer rate is 128 samples × 32 bits/7.8ms ~ 0.525Mb/sec.

In the next chapter, we will try to speed that up by using *inline assembly instructions*.

15.6 Summary

We can access all the same registers as in Spin or PASM. In particular, we can write to the outa and read from the ina registers thusly (Listing 15-8):

Listing 15-8. A C language template for setting and reading a pin

```
1  #define INPIN 0
2  #define OUTPIN 16
3
4  int main() {
5    const inPinMask =(1U << INPIN);   // create masks with ↵
                                          pin position = 1
```

```
6     const outPinMask =(1U << OUTPIN);
7     int i, inVal ;
8
9     DIRA |= outPinMask ;  // set the direction for OUTPIN ↵
                                to output
10    DIRA &= ~inPinMask ;  // ... and the directino for INPIN ↵
                                to input
11
12    for (i=0; i <10; i++) {
13      waitcnt (CNT + CLKFREQ);  // access the CNT register ↵
                                  and the CLKFREQ value
14      OUTA ^= outPinMask ;       // toggle the OUTPIN value
15      inVal = (INA & inPinMask) >> INPIN ;  // read the ↵
                                              INPIN value
16      printf (" inVal = %d\n", inVal);
17    }
18
19    while (1) {
20      waitpeq(inPinMask, inPinMask);  // wait for INPIN to ↵
                                        be high
21      printf(" switch pressed ...\ n");
22      waitpne(inPinMask, inPinMask);  // ... and low
23      printf(" switch released ...\ n");
24  }
```

Here are some valuable fragments of C code:

```
1  bitValue = 1;
2  mask1 = (1U << bitPosition1 )
3  mask2 = (1U << bitPosition2 )
4  reg |= mask1 ; // set a bit at bitPosition1
5
```

```
 6  // set a bit in reg at bitPosition1 and bitPosition2
 7  reg |= ( mask1 | mask2 );
 8  // clear the bits at bitPosition1 and bitPosition2
 9  reg &= ~( mask1 | mask2 );
10  reg ^= mask1 ; // toggle the bit at bitPosition1
11
12  // set the value of the bit at bitPosition1 in variable
13  // reg to the value of bitValue
14  reg ^= (- bitValue ^ reg) & mask1 ;
15
16  // read the value of the bit at bitPosition1 of variable reg
17  bitValue = (reg & mask1 ) >> bitPosition1 ;
18
19  // shift the value of bit 0 of bitValue into reg
20  reg = (reg << 1) | ( bitvalue & 0x01)
```

There is no equivalent to the sar (or "shift arithmetic right") instruction whereby when you shift right and the high bit is copied into the shifted positions. Rather, we must use a C construct known as a *bitfield*.

```
 1  // Spin or PASM :
 2  // i := $FF ' i is %00000000 _00000000_00000000_11111111
 3  // i <<= 24 ' shift left by 24 bits
 4  // now i is $FF_00_00_00 or %11111111 ↩
        _00000000_00000000_00000000
 5  // i ~>= 24 ' shift arithmetic right by 24 bits
 6  // now i is $FF_FF_FF_FF or %11111111 ↩
        _11111111_11111111_11111111
 7
 8  // C:
 9  int i, signExtendi ;
10  i = 0xFF;
```

```
11  // i is %00000000 _00000000_00000000_11111111,
12  // which is i =255 if treated as a 32 bit number,
13  // but i=-1 ** if treated as an eight -bit number **
14  // we would like to set signExtendi to be a 32 bit value ↵
    equal to -1
15  //
16  // One can inform C of the bit - size of a number by ↵
    creating a
17  // struct with a field that has a ":8" (for an eight bit number)
18  struct signExtend8 {
19      signed int x :8; // the :n can be any number ...
20  } s8;
21
22  // we assign our signed eight bit number 0 x000000FF to ↵
    the bitfield
23  s8.x = i;
24  // ** when we ask for it back and want it written to a ↵
    32 bit number, the
25  // compiler knows to sign extend it properly **
26  signExtendi = s8.x;
27  // now signExtendi = 0 xFFFFFFFF
```

CHAPTER 16

Using Inline Assembly Instructions in C Code

Let's now look at using PASM and C in the same stretch of code using a technique called *inline assembly*. You can use this when you require the fastest possible execution of a small section of repeated code. The main part of the code remains in C, but the critical section is written in PASM. In Figure 16-1, there is a drawing of the Antarctic Snow Cruiser: a hybrid exploration vehicle that was ahead of its times.

In this example, we will read the input pin MISO 32 times and shift the value into a variable called val. This is done in SPI (see the previous chapter) where data is transferred serially, one bit at a time.

Here is how we did it in C:

```
1   // get value of miso pin and put it in low bit
2   bit = (INA & MISOMask) >> MISO ;
3   // shift bit into val
4   val |= bit << j;
```

If we were to do this in PASM, we would use the following instructions:

```
1   test ina, misoMask wc ' set C to the miso pin value
2   rcl val, #1           ' rotate val left and set LSB to C
```

© Sridhar Anandakrishnan 2018
S. Anandakrishnan, *Propeller Programming*, https://doi.org/10.1007/978-1-4842-3354-2_16

The PASM code is faster because there are only two instructions to perform, but the C code has six: the AND of INA and MISOMask, the right shift by MISO bits, the assign to bit, the assign to j, the left shift by j, and the OR with val.

We can *inject* the PASM instructions into the middle of the C code to improve performance, as shown in Listing 16-1.

Listing 16-1. Modified Version of spiMaster.cogc That Uses Inline Assembly

```
1   ...
2
3           // get value of miso pin and put in low bit
4           // bit = (INA & MISOMask) >> MISO ;
5           // val |= bit << j;
6           __asm__ (
7             " test %[mask], ina wc\n\t"
8             "rcl %[val], #1\n\t"
9           : // outputs
10            [val] "+r" (val)
11          : // inputs
12            [mask] "r" (mask)
13            );
14          ...
```

- **Lines 4–5**: The commented-out C version of reading MISO.

- **Lines 6–13**: The inline assembly *injection* of the two PASM instructions.

16.1 Inline Assembler

Let's try to decode that gobbledygook!

The inline assembly has the pattern shown in Listing 16-2.

Listing 16-2. Inline Assembly Format

```
1  __asm__ (
2     "<pasm instruction>"
3     "<pasm instruction>"
4   : <output variable>,
5     <output variable>
6   : <input variable>,
7     <input variable>
8  );
```

PASM instructions are standard instructions, with one difference: any variables you want to use in the instruction are referred to as %[<varname>]. These variables can be shared with the C code. This is done via the output and input sections (after the colons). Each PASM instruction is enclosed in quotes. Successive PASM instructions should not have commas, but they can be on different lines.

You can have more than one input/output variable separated by commas. Let's look at lines 7 and 8 in Listing 16-1 in detail.

- test ina, %[miso] wc: test is a PASM instruction with two arguments, and we specify a wc effect. What it does is compare the bit of miso that is high (bit 12) with ina and set the C flag to 1 if ina is 1. The expression %[...] will refer to the variables named in the input and output sections.

- `rcl %[val], #1` will shift the variable `val` left by 1 bit and will shift C into bit 0.

The variables `%[miso]` and `%[val]` refer to the variables `miso` and `val` in the C code because of these statements (lines 10 and 12 of Listing 16-1):

- `[val] "+r" (val)`. This says the variable `val` in the C code should be given the name `val` in the PASM code so that PASM instructions can refer to `%[val]`. The `"+r"` says that this is both an input variable and an output variable. It is modified inside the PASM instructions, and then that modified value is available to the C code.

- `[miso] "r" (miso)`. The `"r"` says that `miso` is solely an input variable and isn't modified in the PASM.

You can refer to the variables by different names in C and in PASM, but why complicate things? (The C variable name is to the right of `"+r"` in parentheses, and the PASM variable name is to the left of `"+r"` in square brackets.)

Figure 16-1. *Antarctic Snow Cruiser. A hybrid tractor, tank, laboratory, and aircraft carrier for Antarctic exploration intended for use by Admiral Byrd in 1939. Alas, its weight was too much for the snow surface, and it was never used. Popular Science Monthly, v. 135, no. 5, Nov., 1939.* `http://bit.ly/2eJOofM`: *public domain.*

16.2 spiSlave.cogc Inline Assembly

The spiSlave.cogc C code can also be modified to use inline assembly, as shown in Listing 16-3.

Listing 16-3. Modified Version of spiSlave.cogc to Use Inline Assembly

```
1   ...
2       // bit = (val >> j) & 0x01 ; // get jth bit
3       // OUTA ^= (-bit ^ OUTA ) & MISOMask ; // set miso pin ⏎
        of outa to bit
4       __asm__ (
5         "shl %[val], #1 wc\n\t"
6         " muxc outa, %[mask]\n\t"
7       : // outputs (+r) for inputs
8         [val] "+r" (val)
9       : // inputs
10        [mask] "r" (mask)
11      );
12  ...
```

- **Lines 2–3**: Commented-out C code that set the MISO pin.

- **Lines 4–11**: Injected PASM code to replace the C code.

- **Line 5**: shl %[val], #1 wc will set C to the most significant bit of val.

- **Line 6**: muxc outa, %[mask] will set outa to the value of C at those bit locations specified in mask.

- **Line 8**: val is a C variable that will be modified by PASM instructions.

- **Line 10**: mask is an input variable only; it isn't modified here.

16.3 Timing

Running this version of the code results in the following:

```
master id = 1 slave id = 2 sem = 1
Time to read 128 longs = 334128
i=0 data=0
i=1 data=1

...
```

This is about twice as fast as the C version.

16.4 Summary

The ability to *inline PASM code* brings an impressive increase in speed while still allowing us to use regular C code for the majority of the work. To use this technique, include an assembler directive at the location where the time-consuming (or bit-twiddling-intensive) code is present.

```
1   ...
2   // c code here
3   int i, j;
4   i = 12;
5   __asm__ (
6     "mov %[j], %[i]\n\t" // the \n is needed to separate the
7     "add %[j], #42\ n\t" // two instructions. The compiler ⏎
                            copies these
8                          // verbatim and without the \n it ⏎
                            would see
9                          // ``mov j, iadd j, #42''
10                         // which is a nonsense instruction
11  : /* output variable j is modified in the asm */
```

```
12    [j] "+r" (j)
13  : /* input variable i is not modified */
14    [i] "r" (i)
15  )
16  // c code continues
17  // here, i is still 12, but j = 54
```

CHAPTER 17

Concluding Thoughts

This book has just skimmed the surface of the capabilities of the Propeller microcontroller.

As always, the best way to learn is by doing, so pick a problem of interest and have at it. The next best way to learn is to study somebody else's code. You can download a number of Spin and PASM projects at the Object Exchange (http://obex.parallax.com).

There are a number of programs already written in Spin, and there is a large knowledge base available to help with learning it and fixing problems. However, Spin is relatively slow. Furthermore, Parallax is encouraging new users to learn to use C to program the Propeller and encouraging existing users to migrate. There is a huge knowledge base of information on "standard" C, but the Propeller-specific parts of C are still in development. Finally, PASM is by far the fastest way to run your code (particularly for bit-twiddling), but Cog-C mode is nearly as fast (see Table 17-1).

Table 17-1. *Comparison of Compression Speeds*

Language	Number of Counts to Compress 128 Samples
Spin code	1.5 million counts
C code (LMM only)	150,000 counts
Cog-C mode	42,000 counts
Mixed-mode C and PASM	23,000 counts
PASM code	22,000 counts

© Sridhar Anandakrishnan 2018
S. Anandakrishnan, *Propeller Programming*, https://doi.org/10.1007/978-1-4842-3354-2_17

The ideal combination may well be C with Cog-C modules and injected inline assembly code for particular tasks. This is also, unsurprisingly, somewhat complex. I hope that you can use the examples in this book to do your own projects. Good luck with your journey (Figure 17-1)!

Our motto might be "Render unto C that which is C's and unto PASM to twiddle bits!"

Figure 17-1. *Crossing the timber line, Pike's Peak Railway, some time between 1898 and 1905. Detroit Photographic Company, public domain.* `https://goo.gl/dzvSXN.`

Index

T, U, V, W, X, Y, Z

Get the eBook for only $5!

Why limit yourself?

With most of our titles available in both PDF and ePUB format, you can access your content wherever and however you wish—on your PC, phone, tablet, or reader.

Since you've purchased this print book, we are happy to offer you the eBook for just $5.

To learn more, go to http://www.apress.com/companion or contact support@apress.com.

Apress®

Made in the USA
Monee, IL
20 March 2020